OPPORTUNITY
IS EVERYWHERE

Opportunity

Is Everywhere

The Story of
America's Supermarket Banker

J. ALTON WINGATE

Published by Interview You

Athens, Georgia

www.interviewyou.net

Grateful acknowledgement is made to The Northeast Georgian
for permission to reprint from previously published material the remarks
from Former Governor Roy Barnes, Robert Ingle,
and Governor Sonny Perdue that appear on the dust jacket.

ISBN 0-9773365-2-2

Printed in the United States of America

FOR LINDA

Contents

CONTENTS *continued*

AFTERWORD

APPENDIXES

IN THE PRESENCE OF AN ENTREPRENEUR EXTRAORDINAIRE

IT WAS MY VERY GREAT PRIVILEGE to interview J. Alton Wingate several times in the last months of his life. He reminisced openly; reviewed his extraordinary career in detail; explained community banking and deregulation to me; demonstrated his leadership skills as he handled miscellaneous business matters; offered a glimpse into the extraordinarily close and vital relationship between him and his wife, Linda, by sharing one of the interview sessions with her at their home; candidly answered questions about behind-the-scenes maneuvers; and never let me leave Cornelia without a gift that had the name of the bank or of FSI on it. He was ready to have his story told and was, I think, aware that his story would be one of his many legacies.

Through those days and hours, I often forgot that he was ill, and I think and hope he did, too. He laughed as he told stories of various adventures; I could see him as a young man, collecting the inner tubes that form the centerpiece of the classic Alton story that demonstrates that even as a child, his entrepreneurial spirit never took a vacation. As he recounted his adventures as a collector of overdue accounts when he was a young banker, it was easy to picture the energy, charm, vigor, and strength of his conviction that he was in the right that made him so successful.

His gentlemanly qualities never failed. He always insisted on seeing me out, even if that meant leaving his office or home to drive ahead of me so I would find my way. I was in awe of his insistence on one occasion when it was clear he was having a bad time that day with his illness.

Many names of beloved family, friends, and colleagues came up in the course of the interviews. Interviews with and statements from some of these people are in this book, beginning with an introduction by Howard Hess, Alton's close friend during recent years, and ending with an afterword by his long-time friend Dennis Cathey. You will find others placed throughout the narrative, and we hope you will find, as we do, that it is a pleasure, for instance in several cases, to hear a story from Alton's perspective and then hear parts of it from another person who was involved with the events. What emerges is a portrait of a wonderful man who lived a wonderful life and did not stop to put some of the pieces together until the very end of that life. We witness his surprise as he realizes just how all-encompassing his desire to achieve and to help people and to grow enterprises was, that it was always there, right from the start. One thing he always recognized and was grateful for was the help and encouragement of family, friends, and mentors. Through Alton's words and additional material by some of his friends, we get a chance to look behind the curtain, see the work, preparation, and sometimes pain that it took to make certain things come to be as this entrepreneur extraordinaire brought dream after dream to life.

Unfortunately, though most of us never wanted to get off the hope train that Alton was driving, he did not live to review this book. Thus, any errors of fact or of any other kind are not his fault. He does – and he would say his family and his Christian upbringing, his friends, and those he worked with – bear responsibility for the extraordinary business success and the goodness, prosperity, and kindness he made happen through his life and for any value this book may hold.

Donna Maddock-Cowart
Interview You, LLC

OUR FRIENDSHIP GREW TO BROTHERHOOD

BY HOWARD HESS

Senior Vice President and Regional Director, Retired
Winn-Dixie Stores, Inc.

THINKING ABOUT ALTON WINGATE, I noted some qualities that were at the heart of his character. First are his integrity and his business ethics. So many times I've heard him say, "That's not right." And the list of qualities goes on. His sense of responsibility for his community, state, and nation. His Christian faith and good works on earth. His never forgetting his roots and those who helped him along the way. His love of family and family heritage. His belief in the law of reciprocity: Give generously, and it will return to you in some form at some time in an enhanced state. His hundred-dollar handshake to guys when he felt this was needed for their families. He'd do this handshake at any time, especially holidays. He'd just go up and say, "Hey, partner, Merry Christmas to you and your family," and in the handshake he'd transfer a hundred or even two-hundred dollars. I've seen that happen so many times.

His courageous stand on his battle with cancer. He was always optimistic. He was always saying, "I'm going to win the battle." His kindness to health-care persons. I visited him in the hospital, and he was passing Susan B. Anthony's and gold coins to all those who were helping him. His telephone greeting and personal greeting was always, "Hey, partner!" His love of hunting clothes and hunting gadgets. Anything new in hunting gadgets or clothes, Alton would buy. For example, he bought a toe rest for a gun that went into the lace of your shoes – skeet shooters use it to rest their gun – and he took it quail hunting. He bought a stirrup sling for the butt of the gun that you put around your neck and then you put the gun in to ease the weight as you walk the woods. His guns – his first gun was a camouflage pump turkey gun that his wife had bought him. When he first started hunting, the clothes he'd wear were just basic leisure; over time he became the best dressed hunter and owned a great collection of purchased shotguns along with several his bank employees gave him.

* * * * *

This is how our friendship began. In the winter of 1986 my superior called me in Louisville, Kentucky, where I was division manager of the Louisville division serving the Kentucky, Nashville, Tennessee, and Southern Indiana area. He informed me that he was sending Mr. J. Alton Wingate to Louisville the following week to present in-store banking to us. He said Mr. Wingate was the father of supermarket banking and carried that title.

The day of the presentation we had a major snowstorm move into our operating area. With all storms there are decisions to be made, including transportation, shipping, receiving, do we load perishables, do we hold, can we ship some areas, hold others, computer scheduling for orders and inventory, etc. We were in constant communication with state road officials and the highway patrol. We'd pull ads, change ads, debate how we could restock the stores and not miss sales. We'd discuss when to close the office and send associates home, how to communicate with all the warehouse and transportation people on coming to work or staying home, etc. And with all this taking place, Alton had flown in for his presentation. I was informed he was in the conference room awaiting me and our real estate man. He made a wonderful presentation. When he finished, I commented that he had a great concept; however, I was in charge of keeping the fat out of the equation, and I had decided that we would try an in-store bank without him as the middle man. At that point I left the room and headed back to the current storm problems.

Mr. Wingate was snowed in at the airport and had to spend the night in Louisville. My superior called him in a couple days and asked him how it went. Alton said, "That's a tough man you have up there." He had asked me also what I thought of it, and what I said was all positive: Alton was very nice, very aggressive, and was just beginning to learn how to make presentations to supermarket people. My superior remarked that both Alton's perception of me and my perception of Alton were wrong.

Several weeks passed, and I got a phone call from my superior, extending an invitation to go quail hunting in south Georgia. My superior was a master of human psychology. When I arrived for the hunt, Mr. Wingate was there. We were assigned to share the same room. We were assigned to sit side-by-side at meals. We were assigned to hunt together. Needless to say, at the end of the outing, we both had a different, improved perception of each other.

And here's the postscript. After a year of trying to establish a bank within a supermarket to no avail, I called Alton and said, "Mr. Wingate, would you please come to Louisville to present your program again?" He complied, and the rest is history.

From the aforementioned events evolved a friendship that words cannot describe. We had a deep respect for each other as businessmen and much respect for each other as individuals. Our company was restructured in June of 2000; I joined the ranks of the retired. This provided an opportunity to grow our friendship from outside the business world of the supplier-customer relationship.

Again, words cannot convey the strength of our friendship. We created lasting memories and enjoyed each other's families, friends, and activities. We hunted, fished, brainstormed, traveled, enjoyed NASCAR activities, and bought the same style Harley-Davidson Dyna Low Rider with identical accessories on the same day. We enjoyed riding in the beautiful north Georgia mountains several times. Rarely a day passed when we did not talk on the phone, no matter what part of the world Alton would be in, conducting business. Our friendship grew to brotherhood. I miss him dearly. When the phone rings I want so much to hear him say, "Hey, partner."

* * * * *

We shared many hunting adventures. Alton was always ready to go, and he set up a lot of hunts. He would always call a hunt a stress-management seminar. Memos would say, "Are you ready to go on the stress-management seminar?" We hunted quail in south Georgia on many plantations; there are a bunch of them down there. We hunted deer in Georgia, Alabama, South Carolina, and Texas. We fished, too – in Georgia, Florida, Arkansas – and Alton fished in Colorado without me. We both fished in Louisiana and Alaska, but not together. We duck hunted in Louisiana and went turkey hunting in Alabama, Georgia, and South Carolina. We went dove hunting in Georgia and Argentina and pheasant hunting in South Dakota.

Alton enjoyed the view of the world from a well-positioned deer stand. Being in a stand well before dawn gave him the opportunity to watch and hear the world wake up. Leaving a stand after sundown provided the opportunity to watch and enter the phase where the nocturnal animals began to move around in search of food. The ride from deer stand back to the lodge always produced sightings of many animals, including deer, raccoons, opossums, and foxes. On a ranch hunting trip in south Texas, Alton and I shared the same hunting jeep. A guide would drive the jeep slowly over many miles of the ranch in search of a nice buck deer with large antlers. On one occasion, first day out, within five minutes after leaving the lodge, Alton spotted a super buck sporting twelve-point antlers. He climbed off the jeep and stalked the buck and within minutes claimed the trophy, the trophy buck of the hunt. This raised the level of the other hunters' expectations. Mine, too. Alton spent the next two days riding with me, trying to spot a buck that would measure up to his. Last day, last hour, we settled for much less.

Alton had amazing reflexes that served him well, and he had the skills necessary to be a great quail hunter. He loved to walk the piney woods and fields of the quail plantations of south Georgia. He honed his skills to become an excellent shot and could shoulder a shotgun and fire it before most hunters could get their guns in firing position. He would have many doubles during a hunt when he was using an over-and-under shotgun, which shot twice. When using an automatic, which shot three times to five times depending on local laws, he would have many triples and several times was able to bring four quail down on a covey rise.

Spring gobbler hunting provides the thrill of watching the world wake up while you are trying to locate turkeys and attract them to your area. Alton loved being propped up against a tree, listening to the birds and watching the forest animals play and move around unaware that he was there, suited in full camouflage, including the face mask, watching their antics. If a turkey showed up in the dogwood-flowered forest, it was extra icing on the cake. If not, the trip to a more peaceful setting to relax, reflect, and enjoy the beauty of our world was well worth the price of admission.

We shared turkey hunts in Georgia, Alabama, and South Carolina. At times we would be spaced several hundred yards apart in a pitch-black 5 A.M. world. As the sun lit up the world, I would hear a shot and think, Alton has taken his gobbler. A few minutes later I would detect a small break in the silence as Alton crawled up to be with me as I tried to duplicate his efforts. After the morning hunt we would enjoy a hot southern breakfast.

Last year after a morning of turkey hunting in Alabama where we enjoyed the hunt immensely without taking a turkey, Alton spotted a large gobbler in the middle of a field on the way out of the woods. The landowner and our guide promised Alton that he would make sure that this turkey would be saved for him for this upcoming season. Alton mentioned the upcoming hunt several times during the past year. That gobbler will long be remembered.

Alton enjoyed fishing very much. He loved the early morning boat ride to the fishing grounds, the beauty of the sunrise on the horizon, birds flying overhead, shrimp boats and oil platforms creating a presence in the Gulf of Mexico; this had a way of draining and cleansing the body of daily and business concerns. Alton would say often, "Partner, relax and enjoy." His favorite spot was the Coco Marina Fishing Complex, near Cocodrie, in Louisiana. Coco Marina provides outstanding facilities, food, boats, guides, and fishing outings. The staff became Alton's friends over the years. He truly enjoyed his stress-management seminars held at Coco Marina. On Alton's first trip there, our guide took us to his favorite spot for catching large bull redfish. Alton had never tangled with a bull red until the guide hollered "Fish on!" and handed him the rod. After a twenty-minute fight with the 40-plus pound bull red, where we had to mop Alton's brow with wet towels and keep refusing the rod from him, the redfish was boated. Alton was totally exhausted in body, but refreshed in mind. Several minutes later he was offering advice to me on what to do as I caught a small bull red.

Alton fished salt water and fresh water. If he had not tried a certain fishing technique, it was just a matter of explaining and showing, and he was on the way to a wonderful experience. Alton fished in Georgia, Arkansas, Florida, Colorado, Louisiana, Alaska, and Kentucky, all with great results.

* * * * *

Alton was one of those people that you never forgot the first time that you met. Ask anyone who knew him about their first meeting, and you will receive a positive, lengthy description of the meeting. When Alton walked into a room, his presence was instantly recognized as that of a very special person. If you did not know him, you would in a short period of time as he worked the room and would speak to each individual and ask questions until he had found a common connection.

Many times I have seen Alton walk into a fast-food restaurant that was running behind and jump behind the counter and help serve or bus tables until they caught up. He loved to return to south Georgia and visit the old hot dog stands from his boyhood days, particularly Jimmy's in Albany. He loved the local barbecue houses and the locally owned and operated southern soul-food restaurants. When the light outside Krispy Kreme was lit, indicating fresh, hot donuts were available, he would make a stop, no matter the time of day or night.

Growing up, he had been a delivery boy for *The Albany Herald*, building his route to legendary proportions and purchasing a Harley-Davidson 165 in the process. Many years later he purchased one of these rare Harley 165's sight unseen from a distant city. It arrived on a large moving van. As soon as it was unloaded, he turned a key and with a swift kick developed years before, made the engine roar to life.

Bringing back the past was very important to Alton. Later, his former boss from *The Albany Herald*, now retired, presented Alton with a *bona fide* canvas bag, a paperboy's shoulder bag just like the one Alton had used as a boy. He was very proud of his paperboy career and had many fond memories from that time.

* * * * *

Alton was always asking open-ended questions to learn about your business and you as a person. He was a good listener and was interested in the whole person and his or her loved ones. He would listen and also share his wisdom and life experiences. When he met people, he would ask where they were from. Once this was answered, he would ask, "Do you know so and so?" until he found a common ground. In banking circles you could always ask, "Do you know Alton Wingate?" and normally the response was, "Everyone knows Alton." He touched many, with most not realizing who was behind the scene or driving the vehicle.

Number one, Alton was a man of vision. Number two, he could read the cards, the lay of the land, the risk/reward ratio and make a sound decision. He had boundless energy for his company, for helping people, and for involvement within his community. He had the entrepreneurial spirit and was willing to share it with others. He believed in the free-enterprise system and proved many times that it worked. As a community banker, he helped grow small businesses within the community. As a community leader, he helped attract industry to his area. As a Christian, he stayed involved in his church and his concerns and never hid his candle under a bushel. He wore and lived his faith for others to see. His good works were many.

* * * * *

Alton was a man's man. It was a great privilege to know him and share life together. His friends miss him very much. We have so many wonderful memories of Alton. When we cross the bar, I'm sure he'll be standing there waiting, smiling and saying, "Partner, what took you so long? Great to see you!"

AUGUST 29, 2005

A gift from Mike Johnston, Alton's close friend since their childhood in Albany

CHAPTER ONE

EXTRA, EXTRA, READ ALL ABOUT IT!

My PAPER ROUTE, MY *ALBANY HERALD* paper route, I now realize as I look back, is what opened doors for me when I was a young fellow.

I was 14 years old when I started officially delivering the *Albany Herald*. My first deliveries were made when I was younger than that, as A. J. Nobles, my boss at the time and a 51-year *Herald* employee, recently reminded me. The *Herald* didn't have a carrier in our neighborhood, and I went and got about ten customers. The *Herald* delivered the papers to me, and then I took them around.

Another friend from Albany pointed out that there was something unusual about my delivery job. "You know," he said, "you were the only one riding a Harley-Davidson on a paper route; you were driving it, and you were only 14 years old."

I didn't start off my delivery career with a motorcycle, though. I started off by delivering the *Grit* on a bicycle. I lived in the country, and I had to ride up and down the highway. The *Grit* was a newspaper that was published somewhere in New York; they cost me a nickel each, and the customer paid a dime. It was a kind of journal, like the *Jacksonville Journal*. It seems to me it was the beginning of what we have today with *USA Today*, just a small version.

I would get all my papers, and they would be good for a week. The *Grit* was a weekly circulation, and I would go out and sell them individually. That was my first paper route. I'd ride my bicycle, ride down a main highway and sell them. I'll never forget one day when I happened to be walking instead of riding my bicycle. I was just walking along, and I looked down and saw a little bundle of money. I reached down and picked it up and put it in my pocket. When I got back to the house, I counted it out. It was five one-dollar bills. That was the most money I'd ever had at one time.

And then opportunity knocked, and I started with *The Albany Herald*. I had my route for seven or eight years, until I had finished two years of college. I was lucky. I had the best paper route in Albany; I built it up to 625 customers, and turned it over to a group of five boys when I left.

I was able to get out of school a little earlier every day because I had a paper route – the *Herald* was an afternoon paper. First, I'd go to the circulation department; I'd work there helping get the papers out that were going all over the south Georgia area. Then they'd run the local paper, and I'd get my papers and start rolling them and packing them up for delivery. When I was delivering on a bicycle, I carried the papers in a canvas bag; actually, I carried them that way even when I moved up to a Harley-Davidson. What I did was I made some adjustments to the bag so that I could put it over the handlebars, using a rubber band to secure it. On the motorcycle, I'd strap it around both sides, like saddlebags.

As my paper route continued to grow, eventually I couldn't get all the papers on my Harley. It was especially difficult on Thursdays and

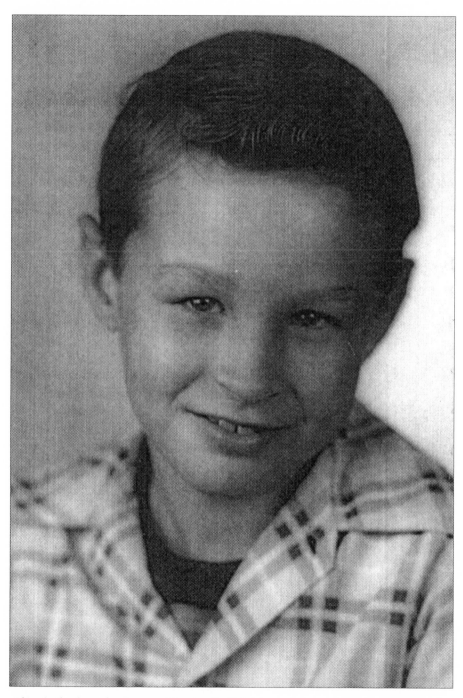

Alton in the days when he was delivering the Grit

Fridays when the paper was larger. At that point, my daddy helped me buy a 1950 Mercury. And that was my first car.

I learned so much about people and business and even basic financial matters on that paper route. Even today, I have many clear memories from that time. Just the other day, the Reverend Jack Tatum came to my office in Cornelia, and he brought his wife with him. I looked at her and said, "Mrs. Tatum, where are you from originally?" (Something about her was familiar to me.)

"Albany," she said.

"Where did you live in Albany?" I asked.

"On Dawson Road," she said.

"How far did you live from the Dairy Queen?" I asked.

"About six houses up from the Dairy Queen," she said.

And I said, "What was your house number?"

She told me, and I said, "Your house was on the right-hand side."

"That's right," she said.

"How did you pay your paper boy?" I asked.

"That was my job every week," she said, "to put thirty-one cents under a flower pot."

"Did you ever see the paper boy?" I asked. "Did you ever see the paper boy pick up that money on Saturday morning?"

"You know," she said, "we never did see the paper boy."

"I'm the one that picked it up," I said.

She couldn't believe it. But that was her job as a little girl, to put the thirty-one cents out there for the paper.

And, of course, I met a lot of my customers not only from knowing their names from the route, but also through the community. Through the church, too – they went to church, I went to church, I met others at the church, and I got to know a lot of people. I had a lot of help. I had so many friends who helped me.

* * * * * *

My customers were so kind to me. I got so many Christmas presents: it was unbelievable. I'd get dollars and shirts and gifts like that. The people who lived on my route were just wonderful people. The man who became my mentor in banking, Cliff Campbell, was on my paper route. He was the one who influenced me to get into banking.

One of my customers had a farm, and he wanted to know if I would cut his grass on the farm in the summer. And I told him, "Sure, I'd be glad to." In the summer when school was out, up until two o'clock, I was kind of free because I didn't go to work for *The Albany Herald* until then. Now, I grew up on a farm, but our tractors did not have power steering. His did, and I will never forget that experience. It was a big difference, and once I mastered the power steering, it was a lot of fun. So I cut his grass on his pasture for him, and we got to know each other a little better. He was a manager of a Coca-Cola plant, and he lived on Dawson Road, too.

I did other jobs for my paper-route customers: painting houses, fences, cutting grass. I had two lawn mowers. There were two boys – Herbie Carter and Marvin Carter – who worked with me just about all the time. Eventually, they wound up getting half my paper route.

* * * * *

One aspect of my time with my paper route is particularly interesting in light of what I ended up pursuing as a career. My sister was head bookkeeper for C & S Bank. She knew I bought me one of these Sears Roebuck little desks, unfinished, and that I kept all my money in that little desk. "You need to open an account," she said to me one day.

"I'm not going to do that," I said. When I thought of a bank back then, I thought of brass and marble and things of that nature.

And that's what I thought of when she said, "Well, why not?"

"I'm not going to go in there with all that marble and glass," I said. She could tell I meant it, and she arranged for me to come to the bookkeeping department and told me she'd get them to open my account in bookkeeping.

So I went to bookkeeping and opened an account with fifteen dollars. The checks were mailed to me, and they had my name on them. I didn't want to write a check. I kept giving her the money to make my deposits for me. I never did go into that bank to make a deposit. ∎

Alton in the days before he made a big decision

A Big Decision

I WAS FORTUNATE IN BEING HEALTHY. I never missed a day in school; I got a 100-percent-attendance certificate every year. I liked to play sports. I loved football. Well, with that paper route, it was kind of tough, but I went out for football. I played on the B team. I had to run and deliver my papers and then go to football practice. And by the time I got to football practice they were all dressed out and ready to go.

On Fridays when we had the games, I had to get somebody to carry my paper route. I'd give the paper route out to two or three other people, and it wasn't easy to get people to deliver those papers. I played fullback, and I can remember scoring several touchdowns, but I was kind of a part-time football player because I had the paper route to deliver. The other guys on the team just went to school and then to practice.

A.J. Nobles, my boss at *The Albany Herald*, came to me one day and he said, "Alton, you need to make up your mind whether you're going to play football or be a paper boy." It was a big decision. I was pretty good because of my size. I weighed about 175 pounds, and I had pretty good speed. (I ran track, too, but the track meets didn't interfere with my paper delivery.) And, of course, playing football was something everybody noticed in high school. While it wasn't easy, it turned out the best decision I ever made was to choose to be a paper boy. ■

A. J. NOBLES

CIRCULATION DIRECTOR (RETIRED), *The Albany Herald*

As you were thinking ahead to this interview for Alton's book, what memories came to mind?

He was such an energetic person, even at a young age. Take, for instance, where he used to live – where his daddy and mother lived – we did not have a carrier that went that far out in the country to deliver the newspapers. He wanted to do something to make money, so he got out in his neighborhood out there and got eight or ten customers. We delivered the papers to him, and he delivered to those eight or ten people, just to get started.

When he got a little bit older, we gave him a paper route, out on the Dawson Road, where he lived, where he wound up his route every day. He stayed on that route through his career with the Herald *and also through his school, his college, and all that.*

He is just a remarkable person.

When he started talking about his life, the paper route came up right away. It was such an important part of his life.

He called me several months ago; he was wanting to dramatize, for his people up there, what he had done to get started in the banking business. He asked me if I had two Herald *bags, like he had when he delivered papers. Those things have become obsolete because most people deliver the papers out of their cars and what have you, and they do not use* Herald *bags at this time. So I got on the phone and I found him two Albany Herald bags. I had to get one from Valdosta, Georgia; one of the former carriers lives in Valdosta, and he had one and sent it to me. Alton wanted me to roll up some papers, some* Albany Herald's, *as they'd been when they went out for delivery.*

Next time I went through Cornelia, Georgia, I went by and left him a big roll of papers and two Herald *bags. He took them and put them on a motorcycle in his lobby there at the bank, and when I went back through there, they were still on display on the back of his motorcycle, like he was fixing to jump on the motorcycle and go deliver them.*

Early in the process of working on his book, Alton was talking about delivering the newspaper, and when asked if he carried them in a bag and what did it look like, he said, "I just happen to have one here," and he brought it out.

Well, that's one of the bags, that's one of the bags.

When I was working on the newspaper, we always worked with schools, trying to explain to the principals and the teachers that a newspaper route was a good education for a carrier, for a young person. (It used to be the paper was delivered by young boys, but now it's gone to adults and retired people.) We emphasized to the principals that it was a good thing for the boys to be able to meet people and learn how to change money, how to sell, and how to work with people. That's what got it into his mind that he wanted to do something like that.

Well, it certainly was important in his life.

It was, it was.

It seems he learned a lot from it.

Well, it's a lot of responsibility. He had to get out every Saturday morning to collect the money and had to pay his bill by twelve o'clock on Saturday. We ventured into the idea of people paying by the month so it would take a lot of the pressure off the carrier. So most of the carriers paid in advance, paid to the office on the fifth of each month. But along those lines, we also instigated – we were the only newspaper that did this – we encouraged the carriers to put up at least five dollars or ten dollars a month, when they paid the bill, for a savings account. And then at the end of the year, if they left the money in there, the Herald *paid them interest on it, from eight to eleven percent interest at that time.*

Wow.

It was a good incentive for them to save money, and Alton was real careful about money. He would put up as much as he could and then when he left – when he got through with his schooling and what have you – and was ready to get a full-time job and so forth, he had enough money to start out.

Isn't that wonderful!

And that's when he got started in the banking business.

It's also how he established credit. He said he had been putting that money in regularly and had almost forgotten it, and then when he was checking out –

He suddenly realized he had it. Well, we had several carriers that when they got through had enough money to pay down on a house or something like that. They had forgotten about it and just had made the payments as a formality; they had to save every month. And we were the only newspaper that gave the carriers interest on what they saved. What I did was I took the money and put it in a savings and loan association – there are two of them here in Albany – well, three of them at that time – and what interest they paid us, we gave it back, all of it, back to the carrier.

Oh, that's great.

So, therefore, if a carrier came in there and he stayed on a route seven months, he didn't get any interest. But the old carriers, that stayed on a route like Alton did, they reaped it all; therefore, they got about eleven percent interest.

You probably could tell a lot of stories about people who started understanding business by being a carrier.

People don't have the youth in mind today like we did then. I had a publisher, James Gray – it was an independent-owned newspaper – who let me do whatever I wanted to as far as the carriers were concerned.

What memories do you have of Alton as a young man? You said you've known him since he was about eight years old?

I believe he was about eight.

What memories do you have of him when he was very young?

Well, I knew that he was real loyal to his family. He was a Christian boy, and his mother and daddy made sure he went to church. He was always a good person; it's a good family. In fact, his brother and I are good friends now.

He feels fortunate in his family; that's clear. Looking back, it seems a decision you told Alton he had to make when he was in high school was truly a major decision for him: that was when you told him he needed to decide between his newspaper route and football.

Oh, yes.

Do you remember that?

Oh, yes. They had to practice in the afternoons. For his paper route – we were the afternoon newspaper – he had to be at the Herald substation about 3:30 in the afternoon, and he was supposed to start practicing ball at 4:00. And I said, "There's no way you can do both of them. Unless your coach will let you come in at 6:00 and start practicing. You have to deliver your newspapers first." He chose the newspaper over football.

Right. Do you recall what brought you to speak to him about it? I think maybe he had been trying to get other people to substitute.

He tried to have a substitute, if my memory is correct, but a substitute does not put the full effort to it that a regular carrier puts to it when it's his regular route. Alton had to sign a contract that he would make sure the paper was delivered by a certain time every day; a substitute on a route doesn't feel loyal to those conditions so they might not deliver on time.

You might be interested to know that when he was talking about the decision, he said that you said, "Alton, you've got to make up your mind whether you're going to play football or be a paperboy." Thinking back on it, Alton said, "Well, it turned out the best decision I ever made was that I decided to be a paperboy."

He was one of the best paperboys and may be one of the best persons I've ever known, to be honest with you. I wish all the young people now had to go through the experience Alton did. He had a father who was real strict; he honored his father all the way, in fact his whole family, his mother and father. He was always loyal to them, and when they said do something, he did it.

When we started our second interview, he began by saying, "I guess I'd better tell you my real name."

Well, I was just fixing to get into that.

Oh, good. He said you still call him Anilton.

I'm about the only one that does. One day, back when he was a carrier, I called his house and asked to speak to Alton Wingate. His sister got real upset about it. She said, "I want to let you know his name is Anilton." It wasn't but a few minutes, and she was down at the Herald. *She said, "This is the way he spells his name, and this is what I want him called." I guess I'm still the only one that calls him Anilton.*

It seems to go along with his principle of making things easy for people – if something is going to be hard for people, he's going to change it.

Well, I was surprised when I saw his name at the bank there, A – l – t – o – n.

Let's talk for a bit about the Jacksonville Beach trips. Do you think he won more of them than anybody?

He did, I believe. What the Herald *did, we sent about 10 boys from the city and 10 from what we called our state. And in order to win this trip – it went on a point system. Let's say the contest ran 13 weeks. The first week you'd start off with 130 points and then it decreased 10 points each week. So if he went out the first week and got 10 new customers, that would mean he got 1,300 points. And the next week if he got 10, he only got 120 points for each one of them. The carrier that got the most points won the trip to Jacksonville. We put this on for about 15 years when I was circulation director.*

That was quite a prize for young people.

And, Alton, I think I figured up he won about 10 of the 15.

I'm not surprised.

You mean so much to him even today; obviously you've stayed in touch over the years. As you watched his career from your vantage point, what are some thoughts you have had about his success?

The only thing I can say about it is that when he takes on a job, he puts his whole heart into it. He's kind of like I was at the Herald: *where you are supposed to put 8 hours in, I'd put 12 hours in, and that's the way he did. I think he put his whole effort to it, and that's the reason he has accomplished as much as he has. Anything that he could do for the person he worked for so that they could better understand him, he did it. That's the way it was at the* Herald *and throughout his bank career. And he takes care of things. Once when we were coming through Cornelia, he made arrangements for us, he got us a suite, had a big bowl of fruit in the room to welcome us, and we had dinner together that night. The next morning he picked us up and took us to the bank and had breakfast served at the bank for us and gave me a tour through the bank.*

When he started those banks in the grocery stores, that was the big, big asset to him to getting wound up in the banking business. I think that's what really excited him, the fact of having people come in and make a quick deposit or whatever. He took me to the first one he did there in Cornelia, and it was a real nice little bank right there in the grocery store, and he explained to me what he was doing.

It shows his focus on the receiver of the services and what's best for them.

Well, the convenience for them and also for the store – it was an asset to the grocery store.

Right. It increases the customer count for the grocery stores.

When he left his paper route and got started in banking, what did you think?

I thought that he was doing the right thing. He had already been through school, he had his schooling, and he had made his mind up what he wanted to do and where he wanted to focus his energy. I thought that was great.

Any other thoughts or comments?

Well, looking at my notes, the last thing I put down is this: He was a leader among other young people in his youth and when he was growing up, and he's still a leader among his peers now. He has always been trustworthy and loyal to his friends, a good Christian, and someone you could depend on in any kind of business situation and in community life. He's the type of person you would want your children to grow up to be – to be something like him.

JULY 23, 2005

Alton's parents, James Leonard and Ida Lois Hatcher Wingate

CHAPTER THREE

MY FATHER BELIEVED IN HELPING PEOPLE

M Y PARENTS WERE CHRISTIAN PEOPLE, and they brought me up in a Christian environment. My dad had a good reputation and, thus, gave me a wonderful name; I recognized the value of a good reputation at an early age and understood that if that was all that he could give me, that was more than enough. And my mother, she was a wonderful person, just a wonderful person. They provided for me; they supported me 150 percent. They always encouraged me; they never once failed to give me encouragement. I lost my parents when they were 60 years old. They were ten years apart in age. I lost my dad when I was in high school. I lost my mother in 1967, a year after I moved to Cornelia.

My parents both grew up on farms, as many people did in southwest Georgia in the early part of the twentieth century. While my father grew up on a farm, he was a tax collector. He was a tax collector for Worth County, and his background was basically working on a farm and collecting taxes for the county.

My father believed in living by the teachings of the Bible as to work and rest: there are seven days; you work for six days, and on the seventh day you rest. So for him and for our family as I was growing up, Sunday was the Lord's Day. My father read the Bible, always read the Bible on Sunday.

He would bring water to the farm hands, and when he would give them the water, he'd have them move to the shade to rest, and he'd say, "I'll turn the plows for you for a while."

But also on Sunday we would visit – visit family and visit friends – and go to church.

My daddy never borrowed any money except one time, to buy a brand new tractor. He believed in paying cash. And, of course, that's unheard of today, paying cash. People generally finance things today. But my father brought me up that way: always save money and pay cash. My sister and brother who lived at home with me were also very thrifty people. My brother got his paycheck every Friday, and the first thing he did was put money in savings. He paid himself first. And then if he had any bills, he'd pay his bills. But he'd always pay himself first. So I had good examples: my parents, my sister, and my brother.

My family consisted of my mother and father, my two brothers, two sisters, and me. My brothers and sisters were my half brothers and half sisters. Their mother passed away when they were very young, and then my father married my mother, and that's when I came along. So I was the youngest child.

But I grew up with a family, not half brothers and half sisters. We never thought of ourselves that way. We were a family. My older brother and my older sister had already moved out of the house by the time I was no longer a baby. So I was raised with a brother and a sister. Both of them

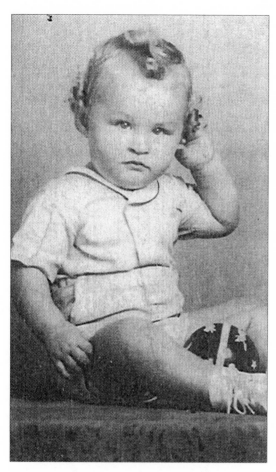

Alton just before he went into business

were not married, so the three of us lived at home with our parents. Before we moved to Albany, my father was a manager of the Putney Estate, which was south of Albany.

I was born in Putney. We lived close to a general store, which was near a railroad track. When I was very young, I remember my mother saying, "Don't you get close to that railroad when that train's coming because if you do it'll suck you up under it." My sister reminded me recently of the family story about how one time when I'd gone down to the store to get some cookies, I'd tiptoed up to the counter and put the money up there. Just then, the whistle of the train sounded, and I could tell the train was coming. Suddenly, like a shot, I took off and headed to our house. I took off and left my cookies there.

My sisters have told me about how my daddy managed that

estate. There were horses and mules to be cared for and farm hands to be supervised. He would bring water to the farm hands, and when he would give them the water, he'd have them move to the shade to rest, and he'd say, "I'll turn the plows for you for a while."

They also reminded me that water was very precious on the Putney Estate, and Daddy always said, "Don't waste the water." Well, we had a large water tank there on the Putney's property, and one of Daddy's jobs was to go out there and check that tank every once in a while to keep the birds out. If the birds got in there, they would mess up the water. So my daddy was climbing up the water tank one time, and he had gone around to the other side, not realizing that I, only four years old, had followed him up the ladder on the tank. About that time, I heard my mother calling. I had climbed up about half way.

When I was four years old, we moved to the Dawson Road in Albany. My father bought a farm. He was a farmer, and he was a builder; he built houses.

* * * * *

My father was a man who believed in helping people, truly helping people. We had cows and we had hogs and we had chickens, and he would loan cows to families that didn't have milk, as well as help out in other ways as needed. He would allow families to take a cow to provide milk for the family. I remember going with him on Sunday afternoons, just riding around and going and looking at the cows. I remember so many times people saying, "That cow passed away," and my dad never did get upset or question them about the loss of the cow. He never got mad; he would just say, "Well, if you need another one, let me know." He was just a wonderful individual.

My father also got a lot of respect from the people in the community because of a special gift he had; he was known for being able to do what is known as "talking the fire out" of people who had been burned. He would have people call who wanted him to come over and "talk the fire out." People said that once he did that, the fire would just kind of disappear.

My father could build houses, he could farm,

Young Alton in his father's arms

he knew equipment, and he also served as a veterinarian. I remember going with him when he was doing veterinary work; I remember that when he'd work on little pigs, my job was to hold the pig. They would be screaming so loud, and my daddy would be there with his little knife and all his instruments, calmly working on them. He was always helping people. He did it for the community.

* * * * *

I never did see my daddy in bed. He was always up and out.

My breakfast was grits, eggs, and a big biscuit with jelly. My mother would always have it in the stove for me when I got to the kitchen in the morning. We always had a big meal at lunch: fried chicken, creamed corn, string beans, butter beans, cucumbers, and sliced tomatoes. Supper would be a small meal, warmed-up leftovers from lunch. At night when we ate together, my father would always say the blessing. And when he would say the blessing, he would get down on his knees next to the table.

Everyone else would stay seated. My father would be the only one who, after everyone was seated, would get out of his chair and get down on his knees to say the blessing.

I can still see us all sitting there around the table and my father saying the blessing, kneeling on the floor nearby. ■

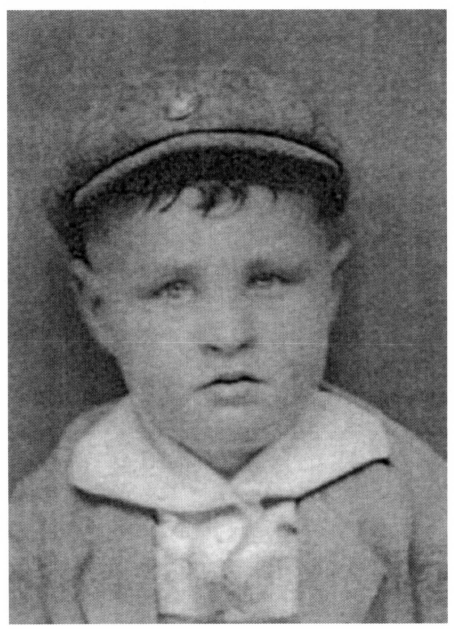

Alton in the days when he was known as Anilton

THAT'S THE WAY LIFE WAS BACK THEN WHEN I GREW UP

M Y REAL NAME IS JOSEPH ANILTON WINGATE. Anilton, not Alton.

It's a family name. I used that name until I realized that people couldn't pronounce Anilton, had a hard time with it. So I told my mother one day I was going to shorten it to Alton. I can't remember when I shortened it, probably when I went into junior high school. So I started using the name Alton. (A lot of people think that's for Alton, Illinois, but it's not.) I've used that name ever since, from my junior high days on up.

My mother had mixed emotions about it, but she said, "If that's what you want to do, that's fine, of course." But now, my immediate family, they call me Anilton and some of my friends from years ago call me Anilton, like A.J. Nobles, from *The Albany Herald* – he calls me Anilton.

* * * * *

So I grew up on the farm, and, as a little boy, I can remember getting up in the morning, playing with my toys – my old John Deere tractor and my Farmall tractor and other toys.

There was an African-American family that lived on our farm,

Porterfield Memorial Methodist Church's first Youth Fellowship president

and one of the children, Joe Jackson, was my best friend. He had a goat and wagon, and we would hitch up that goat to the wagon and play together. When mother would feed me, she'd feed Joe. I never questioned it, but I'd come in the house to eat, and Joe would eat out on the porch. I could never understand that, but that's the way life was back then when I grew up.

I remember getting my first bicycle, a J.C. Higgins bicycle put out by Sears Roebuck, and I remember going down to River Bend and Radium Springs to go swimming when it was hot. Radium Springs was cold water, very cold. We used to go to Cheehaw State Park, too.

When I was growing up and would get up in the morning, my mother would always have breakfast for me. And she would have toothpaste on my toothbrush, all ready for me. (My wife, Linda, says if my mother could have breathed for me, she would have.)

* * * * *

All the members of my family were Baptist. But I moved out of that tradition when I went to Leesburg High School. There was a Methodist church on one end of the school and a Baptist on the other end. When the churches would have a revival, school would be let out, and we could go to the revivals. I remember liking the little white Methodist Church when I would see it as a little boy and then liked going to it while I was at Leesburg High School.

But the main reason I switched over to the Methodists was I had a girlfriend who was a Methodist. She and I started dating in high school. (As far as girlfriends when I was in high school, I had two girlfriends, could possibly have been three but probably two, that's about it.)

Then I was fortunate enough to be one of the charter members of the Porterfield Memorial Methodist Church, which is on the Dawson Road in Albany. We had 126 members; Handy Hancock was the pastor, and he later worked his way up to being the bishop and now lives in Macon, Georgia. One of the highlights of my life in dealing with the minister was when he was new in the area, and he wanted me to show him around town. I showed him around town, and I'd drive him to funerals and things of that nature. He and I developed a very close relationship. And to this day, we're still very close.

I was the first Methodist Youth Fellowship president. I was very involved in the church there, going to services and to other activities, like camp. The first thing we built at the church was a basketball court. Today Porterfield is probably one of the largest churches there. It's down on the Dawson Road. ■

BISHOP 'HANDY' HANCOCK

BISHOP (RETIRED), THE UNITED METHODIST CHURCH

I have known Alton Wingate for nearly fifty years. I came to be the pastor of a new church, Porterfield Memorial United Methodist Church in Albany, Georgia, in June of 1956. Among the high school youth was an active young person, Alton Wingate. He demonstrated a maturity beyond his years. He was a "senior" among the youth. On youth camps, Alton would be like an adult counselor with the youth group.

He was one of the most industrious young persons I have ever known. After school, he delivered The Albany Herald *to residents over a large area. He acquired a car so that he might be able to deliver the papers to an increasing number of residents.*

I seem to remember that there was a young man in the church named Cliff Campbell who was employed by the Citizens and Southern Bank of Albany. He noted the industrious nature of Alton and got him some afternoon employment with the bank. When Alton graduated from high school, he enrolled at The University of Georgia. They were able to get him some employment with the C & S Bank of Athens. After his graduation, Alton was finally able to come to Cornelia and the Community Bank there. I happen to know that he became very active in the Cornelia United Methodist Church as a member and leader. His leadership in the Cornelia community is well documented. I have considered him one of the most self-driven young men I have ever known. If there is such a thing as a self-made man, he just might be one of those persons.

He has always been a wholesome person with the finest of principles. I have admired his character development as well as his maturity. I sense him to be a person of high quality, rooted in wholesome morals and spirituality.

Having been his pastor during his high school years, I am exceedingly proud of him. He has long been motivated to be a person of honor and a success in life. I hold him in the highest esteem.

AUGUST 8, 2005

Visiting the Old Jail in St. Augustine during Albany Herald *prize trip*

CHAPTER FIVE

I Was Always Doing Something

I T'S FUNNY, BUT UNTIL I STARTED WORKING on this book, I never thought about how I was always doing something, always finding opportunities and coming up with something to do. I just never really thought about it until I started thinking back over my whole life.

On our farm we had a scuppernong vine. I picked scuppernongs, and we sold them. We had peas on our farm, too. Daddy would let me plant peas in the corn, and I picked those peas, and we'd sell them, too. I used to buy watermelons for ten cents apiece, and then I'd get those boys that helped me on my paper route. We'd put the watermelons on the truck and we'd go down the street, the boys knocking on doors – seeing if people would like to buy a watermelon for a dollar – while I'd drive the truck along. The watermelons that didn't get sold, I'd put out in front of Merry Acres [a motel in Albany] under the pecan trees that used to be there. People going home in the afternoon would just pull over there, and I'd sell them a watermelon off the back of the truck.

There were lots of other opportunities, too. My brother-in-law Leon Johnson, one of the finest individuals I have ever met, was in school at the University of Florida at some point when I was growing up, and my mother and I and Dad went down there for a Florida-Auburn game. My brother-

People who were visiting the beach wanted to go out on floats and inner tubes, and there were not enough to supply all the people who might have liked to use them. I said, "If I win a trip down there next year, I'm going to see if I can eliminate that problem."

in-law had a scooter, a Cushman scooter, and on Saturday morning I rode it over to the stadium. They were signing up people to sell Pepsi-Colas at the game. The deal was they would give you a foot tub, and you would put the drinks in the foot tub and put the ice on top. So I signed up for that and made twenty-five dollars in one afternoon.

I had my first motorcycle accident on that Cushman scooter. This lady ran into me and knocked me off of it. I didn't get hurt, but it scared the living daylights out of me. But I remember even more clearly carrying that tub around in the stadium, taking it back to get more Pepsi's each time I'd sold all that were in the tub, going up and down the steps. There are opportunities everywhere; all you've got to do is look around.

Even then I believed in marketing, getting your name out in front of people. I signed up to be a representative for a company that made pens and pencils that people would put their company name on to use for marketing. That was another thing I did on the side while I was in high school.

Then, when I got into college, I used to sell Packard shirts, $4.95 for an oxford-cloth Packard shirt with three initials on it. The company was called Packard; it was out of Terre Haute, Indiana. I had a little kit, so I could measure a customer for a shirt.

* * * * *

Another opportunity came out of my job of delivering the *Herald;* the paper held a contest for the paper boys. You could win a week's vacation to go to Jacksonville Beach.

The way you won the trip was by having an increase in subscribers. I was fortunate enough to be on a paper route where I was able to increase my subscriptions. For five years, I would say, I, along with four other boys,

The Albany Herald *prize-winning carriers line up for a photo on Jacksonville Beach. Alton is third from right.*

won that trip.

It was just great. We stayed at the Wymers' Lodge on Jacksonville Beach. I got to know the Wymers, the couple that owned the lodge, real well. One day, I noticed that there was a demand that was not being well met. People who were visiting the beach wanted to go out on floats and inner tubes and there were not enough to supply all the people who might have liked to use them. I said, "If I win a trip down there next year, I'm going to see if I can eliminate that problem."

Well, the next year, it looked like I was going to win, so I started collecting inner tubes, getting worn-out tubes from service stations. I accumulated 600 inner tubes. Yes, 600. Also, I bought nine dollars worth of patches. They came in large pieces, and you could cut out whatever size you needed. And I got ready to carry those inner tubes down there.

First, I talked Mr. Nobles into letting me drive my car to the beach. I told him what I had done and that I had to drive so that I could get all those inner tubes to Jacksonville Beach. He wasn't eager for me to drive my car and not drive with the group. But I thought to tell him that his wife could ride with me so that she wouldn't have to ride with a bunch of boys. I think that's what convinced him. And so he let me drive my car.

We got down there on Sunday afternoon. I told Mr. Wymer what I'd done, and he said, "That's fine, Alton, but you've got to have a license to do that."

"A license?" I asked.

"Yep, you've got to go and get a license from the chamber of commerce."

So, on Monday morning, I was the first one there. I knocked on the door, and they let me in. I told them what I was going to do. My plan

Almost ready to graduate from high school

was to rent the inner tubes out from Monday to about Thursday. (We were to leave on Saturday.) On Friday and Saturday, I was going to sell them.

"You can go ahead and do it, but you have to have a license."

"How much," I asked, "is the license?"

"One hundred dollars."

"A hundred dollars?" I said. "I only need it for a week."

"We're sorry; it costs a hundred dollars."

Well, that was a lot of money. So I went to this Pure service station. I told the guy there what I had and what I had planned to do. "You know," I told him, "you could lease these things out forever and ever. They want me to buy a license and I can't afford it – that's a lot of money. What I'd like to do is I'd like to sell all these tubes to you and you do what I was going to do."

"How much you want for them?" he asked.

"Six hundred dollars."

"Unload them."

And I unloaded every one of them.

So I had made a lot of money and didn't even have to rent out the tubes.

But that's not quite the end of the story. The boys I was with all played cards; they played poker. I didn't know how to play poker. But I had cash. I loaned them money. For every dollar I loaned them, they paid me back a dollar and a quarter.

Someone called it my first loan transaction. That's right. It was just supply and demand. I had the supply, had that cash on me. It was supply and demand.

* * * * *

The St. Louis Cardinals used to be in Albany with a minor league. The ball games were usually at night, after I got through delivering my paper route, so I went out and applied for a job at the concession stand. "First," they told me, "you've got to learn how to chase balls.

"What's that all about?" I asked.

"Well, they knock them out in the park, pow, and you get them and bring them back." The pay for that was a dollar a night.

So that's what I started off doing until I worked my way up to the popcorn popper.

* * * * *

When I grew up, popcorn was available at the theaters and also at the shoeshine stands or the barber shops. You could easily get your shoes shined at the stands or at the barber shops. It was just a part of our community to have those available. In a small community like Cornelia, we have no theater. The barbershops have no place to get your shoes shined. So, at our bank we shine shoes for free on Fridays and Saturdays. We also have free popcorn available. Providing the popcorn and the shoeshine stand for our customers and our potential customers just seemed like a good way to contribute some little extras to our community. Now we pop about 25 pounds a week. ∎

Alton and his brother Stokley (James Stokley Wingate)

CHAPTER SIX

A BIG CHANGE

I KEPT MY PAPER ROUTE UNTIL I FINISHED TWO YEARS OF COLLEGE. When I knew I was leaving my paper route for good, I wrote a letter to my customers. I copied it on a mimeograph machine, and I stuck it in the paper.

Cliff Campbell lived on my paper route, and he was a member of Porterfield Memorial, too. When I told him that I was going to go to Georgia State and I needed to find a job, he asked me if I had looked into going into banking.

"I have thought about it, but not too much about it," I said.

"Well," he said, "why don't you consider doing that and staying in Albany and go to the University of Georgia Center and then we'll transfer you."

Then he described how I would start. "The job that we would offer you," he said, "is kind of a manual training job; we'd start you in collections."

And I said, "I'm interested in doing that."

When he saw how much money I made with my newspaper route, he said, "Well, we've got a problem though. We can't pay you the amount of money that you're making now."

"I'm not interested in the money," I said. "I don't want to be a professional paper boy. And I'd like to get into the banking business and help people."

And that's what I did. I was going to be making a lot less money, but I felt that Mr. Campbell was offering me a better future. So he was my mentor.

And that's how I got into banking. ■

CLIFF CAMPBELL

PRESIDENT (RETIRED), CITIZENS & SOUTHERN NATIONAL BANK OF THOMASVILLE

I was one of the customers on Alton's Albany Herald *paper route, but that's not really where I first knew him. I met him in the late fifties; I went to Albany in 1956. Alton was in high school, and he played football. Also, we went to the same church, Porterfield Memorial Church.*

I was superintendent of the youth division one year, and if a Sunday School teacher didn't show up, I had to teach the lesson. I got to know a lot of the young people, particularly Alton because he was very, very active; he was very much a people person. I saw that.

We would talk sometimes after church, and one time I said, "Alton, you don't want to carry papers all the rest of your life; why don't you come down and talk to me about the bank. I could probably put you to work at the bank." I was running the installment loan department for the C & S bank at that time. That's where our training began for most of the young men that came into the bank. So I knew he'd fit in all right. He said he might be interested.

So he came down to talk to me, and I knew right away that I wanted to hire him if I could. He told me he was trying to go to school at Georgia Southwestern at Americus and carry papers at the same time. I said, "Alton, if I can talk you into coming to work for the bank, you can continue to go to school, and when you get through your two years in Americus, we'll transfer you to Athens so you can finish." It sounded good to him.

I told him, "We could probably pay you $250.00 a month," and Alton looked kind of concerned. He said, "Mr. Campbell, I make a lot more than that carrying papers."

"Well, how about $300.00 a month?" I asked. And he agreed to that, but he was making more than that carrying papers. Jim Gray, who owned The Albany Herald, *was on our board and he said, "Cliff, you hired the best paper boy I had. I had to hire three or four people to take the paper routes that Alton was doing."*

So that's the way we got started, and I put him on as an outside adjuster, as we called them. And the amazing thing about it is, you know, being such a people person that he was, even our "past dues" liked him. And he was very good. He worked hard. He was a very deliberate person and a very hard-working person. He didn't like to be still. He worked outside for a year or so, and then I brought him in and put him in charge of collections on the inside so he could go to school at night.

We had a very proven method of handling the way we sent out notices, the way we assigned our accounts to the outside adjusters, and it was a proven method that was in our operating guide so that as we moved people along, they could come in there and read the operating guide and realize what they were doing and just sit right down in the chair and start doing it. Well, I went by the desk one day, and I saw all of these little tags, different colored tags everywhere on the past-due tray and I said, "Alton, what in the world is that?"

"That's the way I assigned the past-dues out and where we send notices," he said.

"We've got a method of doing this," I said. "Why don't you follow it?"

He said, "I like this method best."

"What about when somebody comes along from behind you, how are they going to know what you've been doing? You've got it all in your head and on those colored tabs sitting up there."

"They can read the operating guide," he said.

"All right," I said, "I'm not going to argue with you. If it works, it works. But if it doesn't, you need to go back to the operating guide." But it did work, and he did that job until he was finished up in Americus. When he told me he was ready to go to Athens, I called the president of the bank in Athens at that time and told him that I'd like to transfer Alton to Athens. I said that he was probably the best man that I had hired in a long, long time and probably the best I've ever hired.

He said, "You know, Cliff, people are always sending me people, these dregs that they don't want."

"This is not one of those; this is a top-notch man," I said. "I'll tell you what, if this man isn't the best man that has come into your bank to work for you, if he's not as good as I say he is, then you send him back down, and we'll reimburse you for his salary."

"Cliff," he said, "I'll take him because that's the first time I've ever had a man sent to Athens guaranteed."

I had a lot of friends up there and, of course, they took to him immediately. After he had been there for four or five years, he called me one day and said, "The Kimseys up in Cornelia want me to come to work up there at the Bank *of Cornelia."*

"Alton," I said, "What are they offering you?"

"Cliff Kimsey says he's about getting ready to retire, and when he retires, I can move up to his slot [he was president]."

"Well, if you can do the job, you take the job up there because if he's told you that, that's what he'll do." We talked; he called me a lot of times and asked me about this, that, and the other, after he went up there. Of course, he got along fine and eventually moved into the slot as president of the bank up there.

He was very innovative and always had something going. We both were on the Georgia Bankers' Board of Directors. I moved up into the chair and became president of the Georgia Bankers Association. We talked one day at a meeting, and he said, "I want to be president of the Georgia Bankers Association. Will you help me?" I said I would, and I did, and he followed me as president of the Georgia Bankers Association, right behind me.

When Alton decided he was going to get into supermarket banks, he called me, and we talked about it. At one point I said, "Alton, I don't know whether this is brand new or not, I'm sure people have thought of it, but if you decide you want to go into it, then you are going to have to work hard to promote it," and he said he realized that. But he had already found Ingles and got-ten connected with Winn-Dixie. He pretty well knew the map that he was going to follow.

Of course, I followed his progress in that and went to a couple of the open-ings that he had in various stores when I could get to them, and then, in fact, my youngest son worked for him in the supermarket banks for a while. He just about ran my son into the ground. He'd call him up on Sunday night and say, "I'm going to pick you up at 6 o'clock in the morning in Valdosta; we're going to Florida." My son was single at the time, and so it didn't make a difference, but he finally decided, he said, "I can't keep up with Alton." They called Alton "the chief." My son said, "I can't keep up with the chief. He's just wearing me out."

I retired in '89. Alton called me one day and said, "You want to buy a condominium?"

"Alton," I said, "what would I do with a condominium? I've got a house up there [in Highlands]."

He said, "Well, this would be an investment." So we bought a condominium together. And he and Linda and my wife, Frances, we went up and bought some furniture for the condominium. We rented it, and we kept it for about two, maybe three years, and we would have negative cash flow on the thing. Finally we just decided to get rid of it, and we put it up for sale and finally got just about what we paid for it out of it. So we didn't make money in the real estate business.

But we went a lot of places together. Once we were in Houston, Texas, for a meeting. My suitcase got damaged, and Alton and Linda kept insisting I go over to Delta and let them look at my suitcase. So I put my briefcase down and we went over to Delta; then we went out and got in a cab and went to the hotel. As soon as we got to the hotel, I said, "You got my briefcase?"

My briefcase was back out at the airport. It was a twenty-five-dollar cab ride back out to the airport. Linda said, "Alton, you might as well go with him because I left my jewelry box and makeup case out there at the airport, too." We were able to retrieve everything. Alton and I were pleased to split the cab fare.

Money didn't matter anything to him. That wasn't what drove him. Having a successful idea and seeing it run to its conclusion successfully was what motivated him, not money.

I was able to hire during my career some great young men; so many of them went on out and were either the number-one man in the bank or the number-two man in the bank. But he was probably the best I ever hired.

He got teased sometimes, got called the coleslaw banker, the grocery banker. But really and truly, everybody wished that they had done something like he did.

OCTOBER 2005

From left: Henry Tison (Alton's sister Veda's husband), Alton, Stokley, and Leon Johnson (Alton's sister Sarah's husband), about 1960

CHAPTER EIGHT

ADVENTURES IN COLLECTING

So I DIDN'T GO OFF TO ATLANTA; I STARTED IN
ALBANY, AS A COLLECTOR. In banking if you don't know how to collect money, you will not make it. If you're going to make it in management,
you've got to be able to collect money. No matter how high you go, you've
got to be able to collect money.

The term for the job I had is now "outside adjuster," but all it was,
was I collected money, to tell you the truth. When Cliff Campbell said,
"Now, we can put you as a collector," I said, "Well, I can handle that; I've
been collecting from 600 customers all my life."

And Cliff said, "I ain't talking about 31 cents a week. I'm talking
about hundreds of dollars."

"I can handle it," I said. And so I got started.

* * * * *

I got lots of experience in collecting money. Once I felt like I knew
what the guy owed, and what it was for and that it was past due, our objective
was to collect the money because we're not in the automobile business, we're
not in the house business. We just want the money. Down in south Georgia
people in neighborhoods could be very protective of each other. You'd go
looking for somebody, and, nobody knew him. They never heard of him. So

I'd say, "Well, I got a check that I need to get his signature on."

All of a sudden it would be, "Oh, you're talking about so and so. He'll be back here in about an hour."

We had to go out and find people. I mean we had to actually literally go out, drive around, and find the people. We had to be detectives. Also, I had a tow bar for if a guy didn't pay.

I remember chasing a guy, and I found his car on the street. I was lucky enough that time in that I could back up to it. So I went ahead and backed up to the car and attached a tow bar up to it. Then I went looking for him. He must have seen me coming; he ran out the back door of the restaurant where he was. He jumped in his car, and he tried to take off. Of course, he couldn't.

A few times I was afraid, like the time one guy got after me with an axe. What had happened was this guy had traded in his father's plows on some new ones, and I was out there to collect for them. The guy's daddy was there. The father and son were standing there in this barn and the son came out of that barn swinging an axe at me. Of course, I backed off and said, "We'll handle this a different way." I got in my car, went straight to the sheriff's office, told him what I was trying to do, and got his assistance.

That was the worst scene I ever had, except for chasing people in a cane patch. Chasing people in a cane patch in the hot summer is unbelievably difficult.

Of course, collecting by seeking the person out wasn't the first step. First, we sent a notice out to the customer: this is past due. They first got a 15-day notice, and then if it wasn't paid in 10 days, the person got a letter. Then if he hadn't paid in 10 more days, he gets a phone call. Then

Mr. and Mrs. J. Alton Wingate, December 26, 1964

Alton playing with Frank, Edward, and Beau, 1968

if you can't catch him on the phone, you go out and find him. That was what an outside adjuster did. I worked for a collection manager. My next job would be to move up to collection manager.

* * * * *

And then the time came for me to transfer. I was very much impressed with the guy who interviewed me in Athens. Mostly, I think, it was because he carried me home with him that night, and he had five daughters sitting around the dinner table. I think it was five daughters. I can't remember exactly. And I remember thinking, "Hmm. I hope he'll offer me a job so I can stay here." He did offer me a job, so I started there. And then I met Linda Hodgkinson; she'd gotten a divorce and moved back to her family in Athens and was working with the bank. I think it happened like this: She was Jake McWhorter's secretary, and when he went on vacation I was moved over to fill in for him during that two week period. So Linda was my secretary for two weeks. And that was how we met.

One of the things my mother told me quite a number of times when I was growing up had to do with marriage. She said, "Son, when you get married, you be sure you don't marry somebody with a lot of children because it's too big of a responsibility." Well, Linda, to whom I've been married since 1964, had two little boys when I met her.

So, for a time my biggest fear concerned telling my mother about Linda. But after all those years of telling me not to take on such responsibility when I got married, when I finally told my mother that Linda had two little boys, I was surprised at her reaction. As I listened to her words, it was like a big rock lifted off my shoulders. She said, "Just remember that you've got to love those boys as much as you love her. If you do that, everything will be fine." And it was.

We lived in Athens for two years. We had a house on Cherokee Avenue in Five Points. ■

ROBERT ODUM

Senior Vice President (Retired), C & S Bank

When I first met Alton, he was probably 18 or 19, just out of high school. Prior to going with C & S Bank, Alton had at least six paper routes. He delivered the papers every day, in Albany, then commuted to Americus, completing college courses. He did this while driving a brand new Thunderbird, which he bought totally with his own paper route money. It wasn't a gift from parents or relatives.

I asked him how he had time to deliver papers, commute, attend class, and study. His only answer was that he'd learned to roll papers so tightly that he could throw them a long way and very accurately. He would drive, steering with his knees, while he was throwing papers out of his window. He never said how fast he drove, but I'd bet it was at least the speed limit.

Alton told me about two more of his early capitalistic ventures, both successful. (I'm sure there are many more that others can tell you about.) While in high school, he made a plan that involved visiting local tire dealers and service stations, collecting tire inner tubes that were to be discarded. He would patch all the tubes that were salvageable, then leave on a planned trip to Jacksonville Beach. There he would again visit service stations and inflate the inner tubes (that charm of his got the free air). Then he would go to the beach and sell inner tubes to swimmers for a few hours, then go be a "kid at the beach." But, unlike the others, he would have money, could pay for his gas, food, and have money when he got home.

The other venture was done at least once, maybe several times. He saw a man parked on a busy street selling watermelons out of the back of a truck. Alton passed the vendor several times and realized that he was not selling his melons quickly and it was getting late in the day. Alton bought the remaining truckload and sold the melons that night and the next day, driving to people's houses that he knew, probably many of his paper route customers. I don't know where he got the truck. He probably borrowed it from the man he bought the melons from. Alton is so polite and easygoing. It's almost impossible for people to say no to him.

When Alton started with C & S Bank, he had to take a substantial cut in pay from his job with the paper. His job title was "outside adjuster," which sounds better than outside collector. This was the beginning job in the 50's and 60's for future loan officers. After a brief training period (where the trainers probably learned more from Alton than they taught), Alton was provided a company car, with a tow bar attached to the back bumper and a receipt book. He would leave the bank early on Monday morning with 150 to 200 accounts assigned to him that were scattered all over southwest Georgia and a few even down in the Panhandle. Alton approached this task the same way that he has done everything: wide open. He would return home late on Friday with outstanding results. Alton surprised many people with his results. He is the best collector I ever saw, which is not surprising now when you look back at his many successes in his wonderful career.

Within a few months the Albany office had one of the lowest, if not the lowest, delinquent loan percentage of the large C & S offices. Alton made a lot of people look good.

A few months after Alton had started, I accompanied him on his outside work to see firsthand how he was doing. I was amazed at how some of our problem customers reacted to Alton. They were friendly, and many seemed glad to see him and usually came up with the money to pay him. In the past I and others had called on the same people and were frequently met with hostility and no money.

At one point, he was driving us down a dirt road at 60-plus miles per hour, leaving a huge cloud of dust. We met another car, going in the opposite direction, at about the same speed. Alton slammed on the brakes, cut the steering wheel sharply to the left, doing the 180-degree spinning turnaround you see in the "cop chase" movies on TV today. As he took off in chase, when I could breathe again, I asked, "What are you doing?"

Alton replied, "That's Mr. So-and-so. I've been looking for him for a week."

Alton caught up with the gentlemen, blew his horn politely, and waved. The man stopped, paid Alton, and told him he would have stopped when they passed if he'd recognized him.

Webster's Dictionary should have, with its definition of entrepreneur, a footnote about Alton Wingate.

Alton is one of those very rare people who has the intelligence, creativeness, judgement, adaptivity, and energy to have been very successful in anything that he decided to pursue.

Alton and I have remained friends but do not get to see each other very often anymore. When I look back on the times we spent together, I remember that it was always a pleasure to be in the company of Alton Wingate.

AUGUST 3, 2005

Alton getting ready to move up in the banking world

MOVING INTO BUSINESS DEVELOPMENT AND ON TO CORNELIA

W HEN I HAD MOVED TO ATHENS, I WENT THERE AS A COLLECTION MANAGER. And since I didn't know the area – not even whether Winder and Cornelia were neighbors – I had to have a Sinclair map so I could manage the routing. I didn't want to get one of my guys going way out of his way in order to get the work done.

That's how I got to know Cornelia, learning about the area in order to do my job. Then we had a customer up here. When our guys came to collect from him, he ran them off. He had had some dealings with Calvin Stovall, so I had to go in and see Calvin. That was when I started to get to know him.

My next step with C & S was business development. I was traveling with another employee, a senior vice president. I was about 22 or 23 years old.

I was in Calvin's office one day, and he said, "Have you ever thought about coming to a small town like Cornelia?"

"You know me," I said. "Yeah, I might."

"Well, you ought to think about it," he said. "Cliff Kimsey might be interested in talking to you." ■

H. Calvin Stovall

Chairman of the Board, Community Bankshares, Inc.

Alton, to me, is one of the most remarkable men I have ever known.

When I first met him at C&S Bank in Athens, I could see Alton was a man who made things happen.

I said to him, "We have a little country bank that's done reasonably well up here in Cornelia, and I think the best thing I could do for you is to get you up here, where you can make a difference.

Alton didn't like the idea of leaving C&S, but he responded by asking me, "What sort of chance do I have of getting a position where I can do something? I've never run a bank before."

I just kept hammering away at him. I told him I believed that there was great opportunity here, if he could earn the trust of our people; and so he agreed to put in an application. Well, Alton simply attracted people with his personality and his vision. He won friends quickly and easily, proved himself to be such a man of principle – and, from the beginning, placed his faith in people, trusting them implicitly to do a great job. And on those rare occasions when a person simply didn't measure up to his expectation, it was a great personal blow to him. I would say that if he has a weakness, it's that he believes in people too much.

He has the ability to absorb knowledge about a lot of things very quickly, but, above all, Alton is an unstoppable salesman with great charm. As the author James Barrie says, "Charm is that quality that if you have it, you don't need anything else; and if you don't have it, it doesn't matter what else you have."

I knew he'd make a difference in the bank, but that he'd also make a difference in the community, and he did, right from the start. His coming here changed the future of this whole area – everything he has touched has experienced transformation: our hospital, community organizations, his church. He has this great vision, and a remarkable ability to communicate it to people around him, regardless of their education or socio-economic background.

When Alton first mentioned the idea of putting banks in supermarkets, I thought he was just crazy. It was an immense gamble that has become his supreme accomplishment. He sees opportunity that is simply invisible to the rest of us – and has the guts to go after it with all his heart.

JUNE 25, 2005

Alton Wingate here, ready to make things happen

CHAPTER NINE

PREPARING MYSELF TO MOVE UP THE LADDER

THE BANK IN CORNELIA WAS DOWNTOWN. Over a period of a year they offered me a job to come up here and be in charge of business development and lending. We were eight million bucks then, eight million dollars, and had been around for sixty-six years. This was in 1966. Today we're 855 million. But our industry has changed so much.

At that time, the bank was primarily being run by a father and son, Cliff Kimsey, Jr., and Cliff Kimsey, Sr. One of them was chairman of the board, and one of them was the president. And we had a total of, I believe, 18 employees. We only had our main office, which was downtown, and then we had a branch, located on North Main Street, where our existing main office is today. I felt that my first responsibility would be to get out and meet the people in the community. I already knew four or five people because of my previous employer, people who lived here. I started acting as a business development representative, and also I was in lending.

Basically, I started from there, building a customer base, and worked my way up. One of the primary reasons for me to come to Cornelia was to expand my knowledge of banking. I was specialized at C & S. I was on the retail side, but I never could see the entire operation of a bank. By coming to Cornelia, I could see the entire operation within one building, and so it would give me a chance to learn the operation of a bank, plus it would put me in a position that if I were given an opportunity to be president of a bank, it would give me that background knowledge.

That was in my mind from the time I started; it was one of the primary reasons for me to come to a small community bank. Well, lo and behold, I met some of the finest directors that a bank could have when I came here.

And I began working at that age, in 1966, preparing myself to move up the ladder. Then in 1977 I was given the responsibility and elected to president and CEO. And I had butterflies as big as the bank building over what I was doing. But with the support of the directors and the existing staff, I began building a team. My first letter to the board was in 1977, and since 1977 I have reported to the board on a monthly basis all activity that has transpired since the last board meeting. And I believed in communicating with the board so they would know what was going on here at the bank. So I began then building a team.

In 1977 we began to talk about deregulation, and I felt like there were two things that we needed to concentrate on to remain a community bank, and that's products and services. And non-interest income. Products and services and non-interest income. So I began to lay the groundwork to develop new products and new services and non-interest income. And from 1977 until the early '80's we developed products and services. That is when I began looking at more alternative ways to deliver all those products and services, and that's when I came up with the concept of putting a bank inside a supermarket.

To go back to the ten years when I had my eye on the president's

"Then in 1977 I was given the responsibility and elected to president and CEO. And I had butterfiles as big as the bank building over what I was doing."

chair while I was learning and developing a customer base, I felt like it was important to get involved in the community. I was a member of the Jaycees and the Rotary Club and the Habersham Chamber of Commerce. I served on a hospital authority board and my church. Those five things, my church, the hospital, the Rotary, the Jaycees, and the chamber, those are the things that I needed to give time to, to get involved in the community. And I've served as president of our local chamber. I've served as president of our Rotary Club. I've served as president and chairman of the board of the hospital authority, and I've served as chairman of the finance committee of the church and as chairman of the administrative board. So I've done all those things. I think an individual needs to give back to the community, and this is what I've done: try to give back to the community.

Our institution is owned by the people in this community here. Our employees are the major shareholders of our company. And I've been very active in all the five things that I've just described, and that has helped me as an individual to have a feel for what's happening here in our community. Our company has been very committed to providing talent and person hours to support many projects within the community here. We've had our employees serve on the board of education. We've had employees serve as mayor and members of the council of the community we're in. And this is what I think it takes to make an all-around community bank.

As I was coming along, I was always encouraged in my activities by the leadership here; that was part of the nature of the enterprise. I give credit to the board and management of the bank that encouraged me; the encouragement I got from the board and the senior management here at the bank is the cornerstone of what I have been able to accomplish.

The officers and the board are elected by our shareholders. My first responsibility is to my shareholders, and my second responsibility is to my board because they're the ones that elect management to serve. And I believe very strongly that communication with our board and keeping them abreast as to what's going on here is one of my major responsibilities because every one of them is personally liable for what happens here at this bank. I made a commitment to them that I would never surprise them if they never surprised me, and I tried to operate on that philosophy.

One aspect of the open communication and accountability was that monthly letter to them. Of course, there were times when there were things I wished I didn't have to tell them or that needed quite a bit of explanation. I guess the biggest news was selling them on the concept of going into a supermarket. Because that was not traditional, to do a branch like that. And I did my homework as usual, talking to each individual director prior to the meeting because not letting them know would mean a surprise coming up in the meeting. Then, in 1981, we formed our holding company. Because in the banking structure prior to '81, the only way that you could acquire someone would be through a holding company. In other words, a bank could not go out and buy another bank; you had to do it through a holding company. That's when we created our holding company,

Community Bank Shares, Inc.

We made our first acquisition in 1981, the bank in Commerce, The Northeast Georgia Banking Company. It was about a 15 million dollar bank, and we bought it up. That was our first acquisition.

* * * * *

When I first arrived here, we were open on Monday and Tuesday, and we were open half a day on Wednesday and on Thursday and Friday and half a day on Saturday. I found myself having a lot of time on my hands, and that's when I talked to the management of the bank and got their approval to make an investment in a tire company. So I became the owner of a tire company here. I had time on my hands. I always wanted to stay busy. And then I got permission to make an investment in a Maryland Fried Chicken franchise. I created a company called Almacken with two other guys, and we were in the chicken business. Yes, I was in the chicken business and the tire business until I was made president of the bank. Then in 1979 I divested myself of the tire business and the chicken business because I didn't have so much time on my hands anymore. But I still know how to get nine pieces of chicken out of a chicken. You buy the chicken whole and then you cut it up.

The tire business, Cornelia Tire Company, included a retread shop and a new tire shop, and we did front-end alignments. Cornelia Tire Company. What having those businesses did for me was to put me in the retail side. It helped me broaden my understanding of small business.

I recognized I needed to have a secretary, and I talked to some friends around here and they gave me the names of two individuals that I should talk to. One of them was Annette Fricks, and another was another lady who lived in Clarkesville. I was doing commercials for the bank, and I was at the radio station on Saturday afternoon, and I called Annette at home. She came in to see me on Monday morning, and you know back then the first thing you'd ask was can you take shorthand, and she could take shorthand. But how I wound up with her, Georgia Natural Gas in Athens had hired her and put her across the street over here. She turned out to be pregnant, and back then she could only work for a short period of time. And when she delivered the baby, she didn't have a job. They didn't hold the job open for her. She wasn't allowed to go back to work, and I considered myself very lucky being able to find somebody like Annette. She has just been elected to the holding company board, and her portrait will be up in the board room of the bank with the portraits of the other board members. ■

COMMUNITY BANK & TRUST
The Evolution of a Financial Institution

1900   Bank officially established as Cornelia Bank. First day of business August 4, 1900.
First day's deposits: $796.31.

1914   The Bank of Demorest (founded in 1891) is managed as a "Branch Bank" by Cornelia Bank.

1919   In December Cliff C. Kimsey, Sr. elected Cashier.

1929   Board discontinues allowing overdrafts.

1939   The Bank of Demorest operating as a separate branch bank is consolidated with Cornelia Bank.

1946   Bank begins making G. I. Loans.

1951   Cliff Kimsey, Sr., elected President.

1952   Interest rate on savings accounts raised to 2%.

1955   Group insurance implemented for employees.

1957   In November the Board adjourns early to have dinner with baseball legend Ty Cobb.

1959   Bank begins charging $1.00 for checks presented with insufficient funds.

1960   In January Cliff Kimsey, Sr. celebrates 40th Anniversary with the Bank; in December a profit-sharing
plan adopted for employees.

1963   In January the Demorest Bank destroyed by fire; in April, F. Jack Adams and H. Calvin Stovall, Jr.
elected to board of directors; first "drive-in branch" opens.

1965   Capital increases to $200,000.

1966   In January, Cliff Kimsey, Sr. named chairman of the board and Cliff Kimsey, Jr. elected president;
in July, J. Alton Wingate joins staff as vice president.

1968   A joint venture in computer processing begins with establishment of Financial Computer Services;
participation in BankAmericard (now VISA) credit card program begins.

1969   Limited Trust powers granted to the Bank. At year end 1969, total assets pass $10,000,000.

1973   Student Advisory Board"/Junior Board of Directors established, one of the first in the nation.

1975   Move into new main office facility on North Main Street.

1977   J. Alton Wingate named President and CEO.

1978   First Automated Teller Machine (ATM) installed in Habersham County

1979   Total assets at year-end are $45,000,000.

1981   Holding Company – Community Bankshares, Inc. – established; H. Calvin Stovall, Jr. elected
Chairman of the holding company board of directors.

1982 Bank opens first of three offices in Clarkesville, Georgia; Northeastern Banking Company in Commerce joins the holding company (now Community Bank & Trust-Jackson with seven banking centers in Commerce and Jefferson).

1984 Full Service Trust Department opens; first Supermarket Bank® opens in Ingles Foodstore; Financial Supermarkets, Inc. is established.

1986 In April bank name changed to "Community Bank & Trust" to reflect "community orientation" and to increase marketability in other areas.

1987 J. Alton Wingate named one of the top 35 bank CEOs in the nation by Bankers Monthly magazine.

1989 Bank began Golden Apple Club for customers 50 and older; at year-end total consolidated assets are $146,000,000.

1990 Acquired bank in Alabama from the Resolution Trust Corporation (former office of Phenix Federal Savings & Loan) now Community Bank & Trust-Alabama with banking centers in Union Springs and Montgomery.

1991 First Supermarket Bank in Europe (for the Banque Populaire de Lorraine, France) opens.

1994 Acquired the Bank of Troup (now Community Bank & Trust-Troup with two offices in LaGrange, Georgia); full-service travel agency "in-house" (Community Travel Services) opens.

1995 Full-service Brokerage Accounts, offering non-traditional investment products, established.

1997 Sun Trust branches in Clarkesville and Cleveland, Georgia acquired; two new in-store banking centers open in Hall County; Employee Stock Ownership Plan (ESOP) and 401(k) plan established.

1998 Full service Express Banking Center opens in Gainesville, Georgia; J. Alton Wingate elected Chairman of the Board & CEO of Community Bankshares, Inc. to succeed H. Calvin Stovall who was named Chairman-Emeritus; purchase of Gemperline-Sherwood Agency completed and new real estate office in Clarkesville opened; Financial Supermarkets, Inc. named provider of in-store commissary banks for the Eastern Division, Southern Area, of the U. S. Defense Department.

1999 J. Alton Wingate, Chairman, President & CEO named first recipient of the prestigious Georgia Bankers Association Chairman's Leadership Award; Financial Supermarkets, Inc. named the exclusive in-store provider of choice by Canada's largest financial institution by assets, the Canadian Imperial Bank of Commerce, and in December FSI announces its new alliance with the Food Marketing Institute (FMI) which names FSI as its preferred provider of in-store banking services; total consolidated assets are $516,150,000.

2000 100th anniversary celebration, A Century of Service. Total consolidated assets $590 million, up 14.4% from year-end 1999.

2001 Total consolidated assets $646 million, up 9.47% over year-end 2000, even though 2001 was a year of economic downturn.

2002 Total consolidated assets rise 8.36% to $700,246,000. Loans grow by 7.81%,and deposits are up 8.03%, to $607,354,000.

2003 Total consolidated assets are $766 million, an increase of 9.4% over year-end 2002.

2004 Extraordinary results, with $843 million in total consolidated assets, up 10% from 2003, loans growing 18%, and a 46% increase over 2003 in consolidated income. Financial Supermarkets celebrates its 20th anniversary.

2005 Board wins Bank Director magazine's 2005 Trailblazer Award; total consolidated assets grow to $944 million, up 12%. Most profitable year in the bank's 105-year history.

"You can't take the human touch away"

PRODUCTS AND SERVICES AND NON-INTEREST INCOME

DEREGULATION WAS TO BECOME AN IMPORTANT ASPECT OF MY BANKING CAREER. The trucking industry was the first industry to deregulate. And then the airlines. And then the telephone industry. Then the banks.

There are two types of banks, state banks and national banks. When I first went into banking there was also the savings and loan or S and L, known today as a thrift, so really we have three types of bank charters: the state, the national, and the thrift. The state charters are regulated by the Department of Banking. The national charters are regulated by the OCC (Office of the Comptroller of the Currency) and the thrifts by the OTS (Office of Thrift Supervision). Our bank is a state-chartered bank.

I believe in the dual-banking system because it gives a person or company a choice, whether to have a state bank or a national bank. And we're regulated by those various regulators, as well as by the FDIC, the Federal Deposit Insurance Corporation. (The FDIC came along in 1933.) We are regulated today by the Department of Banks in Georgia and Alabama and also by the FDIC.

* * * * *

When I went into banking, we offered checking accounts and savings accounts, and a checking account could be a personal account or a business account. The only loans we could make were loans on homes and land and cars and cattle, and that was basically it. Well, the uniform commercial code law went into effect in 1964, and that was the beginning of being able to centralize how you perfected a loan, made it legal, and ensured that all the documentation and details were taken care of. For example, where you used to use a bill of sale, you now had a note and a bill of sale. The regulations just continued to pile up.

Deregulation allowed us to come up with new products and services. Once those laws were passed, we were able to offer different products and services. So we could move from just offering personal checking and saving and commercial business accounts. That's where we began to have the things we have now. Now we've got money market accounts, NOW accounts; we've got all the different type of lending and mortgages. The whole menu of things has changed. ATM banking, Internet banking, the whole works.

Some people saw the opportunities deregulation brought for other entities to get into what had traditionally been banking services and products as a threat to banks. My philosophy here is you can't take the human touch away. We have a certain number of our customers that like to have Internet banking. Of course, you've got these other customers who don't want it. And especially with this identity-theft thing that's going on now. With technology, you know, we've tried to position ourselves to take advantage of these things when our customers want them. ■

Alton Wingate, Community Banker

Preparing the way for in-store banking

THE HIGHLIGHT OF MY LIFE

THE HIGHLIGHT OF MY LIFE IS WHEN I DEVELOPED THIS IN-STORE BANKING PROGRAM. The whole thing has meant so much to me. I did that back 21 years ago.

Thinking about the beginnings of that, I remember doing a study on a department store like Belk's and a study on Sky City, which is like a Wal-Mart or a Kmart. And then I did a study on a supermarket. And what drove me to the supermarket was how many customers patronize a supermarket on a weekly basis. Here in Cornelia, Georgia, we had a number of supermarkets, but the one I did the study on was Ingles. I found out that they had ten-thousand customers a week that visit their store. And I thought that's where we should go; we should design a full-service bank to go into a grocery store.

Again, deregulation made it clear that we, our bank, needed to look for non-interest income and new products or services. And my idea about a connection between grocery stores and banks fit that need. I went to the board and began by saying that I felt we needed to come up with another delivery channel. Then I said that the delivery channel I was thinking of was putting a bank inside a supermarket. Well, when I presented it to the board, the concept that our next branch would be within a supermarket, you could hear a pin drop. They all thought I had lost my mind. Of course, I told them that I had done the study and explained why I felt like our next branch should be in a supermarket. This was the early '80's. It was unheard of then.

I said we'd use our bank as a model to test the concept, and then if the customers responded to it, we would put together a little company and offer these services to other financial institutions. We would act as a consultant, having made ourselves experts in how you put an in-store bank together in a retail environment. Fortunately, they had enough confidence in me to let me go ahead with the plan.

Then I had to get the approval of the regulators, of the FDIC and the Department of Banking. I met with them in their office in Atlanta.

I told them my idea, and said I'd like them to consider giving us approval. They didn't seem to be excited. Basically they said, "It sounds like a branch application." I told them we could do it at a fifth of the cost of a brick-and-mortar branch.

So, in 1980, I visited with a representative from Winn-Dixie, and I visited with Robert P. Ingle, who owns Ingles Supermarkets. I told him that what I'd like to do is share my customers with him, and he'd share his with me.

I said, "I think I can increase your customer count by eight to ten percent; I'd like to put a full-service branch within your four walls."

As soon as the customer-count increase registered, he said, "Where would you like to put it?"

We opened our first in-store bank on January the fourth, 1984. And that was the beginning of giving birth to our non-interest income. I said that if it works what we would like to do is represent Ingles Market

The first in-store banking unit

in bringing other institutions to your stores, and we would charge a fee to the financial institution. That's when we began generating non-interest income.

What I mean by bringing in other institutions is this. We make our money on interest on loans and interest on investments, and the only other income that we have is what we call non-interest, fee income. It's not interest on loans or interest on investments. It's fee income for service that we provide. That's considered non-interest income. That was what I said that we needed to concentrate on: building up that non-interest income and come up with new products and services.

When we help other banks establish in-store banks, our non-interest income would come from what we charge those banks to handle all the details, to go and put them inside that store. As of this year [2005], we've done over eight-hundred in-store banks.

From that day forward, really, I felt like we had a future. We incorporated – Financial Supermarkets Incorporated, (FSI) – in December 1984. And that was the beginning of the in-store banking program. ■

Alton in crib with Beau, 1968.

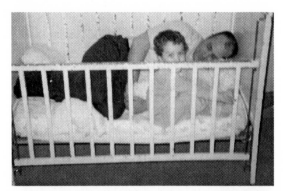

The Wingate family, Alton and Linda with Beau, Frank, and Edward.

Edward, Beau and Frank.

Alton with Alton III, June 6, 2002.

Alton with Alex Odum, grandson of Bob Odum, enjoying an Atlanta Falcons game.

Linda and Alton in the Caribbean.

The grandchildren: (front) Elizabeth, Meredith, Anna Lea, Alton; (back) Caroline, Carlin.

An early trade show display for Financial Supermarkets

CHAPTER TWELVE

BUILDING FSI: COMPETITION IS GOOD

JUST AS I'D PROMISED, WE INCREASED THE CUSTOMER COUNT. And as it happened, in these bank branches, which is what the in-store banks were, we opened more accounts than we did at our brick and mortar branches.

It's building market share. We were trying to come up with the most economical way to build market share, and by going to the supermarket, what we found was a niche.

By now, of course, we have grown and spread all over the country as we moved to developing in-store branches for other banks. We've had the opportunity to go to other countries and develop in-store banking, but I said we need to take care of America first before we go over there.

There's nothing to prevent other banks, of course, from going in and establishing their own in-store banks. Some of them try to do it. My attitude about that is that competition is good for you. What we try to do is basically deliver a quality product and good service. That's what we try to deliver.

What I told Ingles Market was if it works for us it ought to be good for other banks, too, and we'd like to represent you bringing other banks to you. And we work that way with Winn Dixie, Ingles, and Kroger now.

We opened our first in-store bank in January, 1984; I sold the concept the next May, first to a bank in Gainesville. Then we went to Blairsville, Georgia; then to Dallas, Georgia; then Cartersville, Georgia, because that's where Ingles had supermarkets. That was the first retailer that we put together.

We used our bank here as a model, and now we have put it in over 800 locations throughout the United States and one in France. And one just opened in Hawaii.

When we started, we went to Winn Dixie, and Winn Dixie said, "After you've had some experience doing this, you come back to us." In 1985 we went back to them, and they agreed to work with us.

I actually stayed hands-on with FSI for twenty years. I did it because I could see the potential revenue that this little arm would generate up here: it has tremendous potential. We built sales as high as 13 million dollars in a year's time.

* * * * *

We hold annual meetings that draw great participation; they are working meetings, with a lot of information sharing and training. It's a real team effort.

As we began to build FSI, one of the first things we felt we needed was a designer, somebody that could help us design the thing. We needed to have a contractor who could act as general contractor; in addition, we needed to have somebody that could do millwork. There's a difference in millwork and construction. We outsourced. As to organization, we have administrative staff, sales staff, and project-management people. Once we sign a contract, they take it from day one and manage it and put it all

Staying in the midst of the action

together. It's a turnkey deal to the banker. When Kroger, for example, says, "Here's a new store, and we'd like to have a bank," we go out and find a bank. We sign up the bank and get the partner for them as part of the deal.

Once we make a proposal and it's accepted, we design the unit, build the unit, equip it, and turn the key over to them. And then we train the employees as to how to sell bank financial products in that retail bank. That's a big part of it, training.

I've had a lot of bankers say to me, "Alton, this is like a franchise."

"Well, yes," I say, "it is like a franchise, but it's not a franchise approach. We're acting as a consultant to you, to put your institution in a store environment."

People have asked me whether I ran into resistance. Well, it's not something I think about much, but I did run into resistance. Some people said, "It's just going to be a check-cashing center." But, mainly, I have had a lot of support, and, of course, the concept has been successful, so that helps.

I did have to be away from Cornelia a lot, but for us to build the company we had, I had to do that. That was made easier by being able to fly between cities. James Tatum, who manages the airport here, was a very big part in the beginning. We flew together all the time. I introduced James to Albany, and to Jimmy's Hotdogs, one of my favorite places to eat in Albany. I've been buying hotdogs there since they cost a nickel. Now they cost 49 cents. One time I brought some back to the plane, and they were pretty heavily loaded with onion, and that time James said never again bring those hotdogs back with us. Everybody who knew what our flights were like thought that was pretty funny. In the early days, our flying experience was pretty casual. It wasn't unusual to have a dirt dauber's nest inside the plane, and for a while there was a hole in the bottom of the plane. You could look down and see what was below you. But those were good times. With James, I always felt that here's a guy that is on my side.

As the business grew, the planes he flew got bigger. We started off in a very small plane, then went to an Aztec, then a Cessna, then to a King Air. But we did not own a plane back then. Eventually we become part of an ownership plan that ensured that we had access to a plane when we needed it.

We were always part of the community. The town is small enough

This graphic depiction of an old-fashioned grocery store is presented to each FSI in-store bank.

that people would hear the plane coming in, and they'd know who it was. Linda would usually know when I was coming home because we'd fly over the house as we were getting ready to land.

Of course, at first we were just traveling in Georgia and the Southeast. Then we went to Europe. And now we're all over the United States. And we've taken the time we've needed to do it right. I believe in building a solid foundation. First we crawled, then we walked, and now we're taking bigger footsteps. We're all over the United States. The properties that we're marketing for in-stores are all over the United States.

* * * * *

Every FSI bank is given a print of a painting that depicts an old-fashioned store, from a time when the little grocery stores also served as a post office and a basic bank. As a matter of fact, the guy that was trusted in the community was not the banker; he was a grocer. He was the one that provided food and the seed and the clothing and the shoes and also the credit.

The way that the painting came about was that I was talking to a customer of ours who is an artist. I said, "You know, we put banks in supermarkets, and I'd like to leave them with something that is kind of a gift or something." So she began developing a picture that shows that, and I said, "Perfect," and we went from there.

* * * * *

The managers of retail stores claim having an in-store bank increases their volume by as much as 20%. I hear stories, too, about people changing where they shop for groceries once they realize their bank has a branch at a particular store. One of our local business owners told me she'd never shopped at Ingles, always shopped at Winn Dixie or Bi-Lo, but she banks with us. All of a sudden she realized, she said, "I need to do my shopping while I'm here."

Of course, I've always been a believer in the concept. I was so convinced that a banker in Winder, Georgia, would be successful that I guaranteed his investment for three years. "All the money that you put up, we'll return it to you in three years if you're not happy with it." We sealed the deal with a handshake.

It was exciting to learn what I did as the in-store banking concept

The in-store banker

came together. Not every banker has had that opportunity to be exposed to that side of the business world. I didn't realize that the number one retailer in America that attracts customers on a weekly basis is a supermarket. You look at any supermarket, and it's clear that it's true.

Most bankers, when they think of a big retailer, they think of work. I think of a transaction; it's an opportunity for us to turn that transaction around and make a profit. I find it exciting, the way it has worked. I told the stores that we could increase their customer count, I felt like, by eight to ten percent. Well, they knew immediately what that would mean for the bottom line. But we've had reports now that it increased their customer count by twenty percent. And the way they measured that, if the bank comes out of the store, sales would go down.

* * * * *

Just as the organizations I joined when I first came to Cornelia helped me become a part of the community, other organizations that I became a part of as my career progressed were helpful as we built this new business. One was the Conference of State Bank Supervisors. It's a regulators organization, but bankers belonged, too. You're appointed by your commission. I was appointed by the State Commissioner of Bankers, the Georgia Banking Commission: Jack Dunn, he's the one that nicknamed me the "coleslaw banker."

That organization was helpful because I got to know a lot of bankers from all over. Before we would go into a state, I wanted to make sure they knew who we were and what we were offering. ∎

Faye B. Cunningham

Artist & Owner
Faye Cunningham Gallery, Alto, Georgia

Mr. Wingate's heart really was in his community; I thought how fitting it was when they changed the name Cornelia Bank to Community Bank. Community. That was the heartbeat of what he stood for in his work and in his family life and everything connected to him.

Mr. Wingate was a very talented person who enjoyed his work, his family and his life in the best possible ways, with enthusiasm and passion, the kind that filled the room with his open life, his loving and inspiring personality. When he walked in, he was happy and it showed. He brought out the best in people, me included. He inspired people so thoroughly that they actually would do more and perform beyond what they thought was possible. I know from experience that from the beginning of the inspiration to the end result of obtaining the goal that I had in the course of what we did together, there was the pleasure of accomplishment that is hard to measure and even harder to explain.

The most fun thing I did in my career as an artist and art-gallery owner started the day he asked me if I could think of an idea for a painting I could do in connection with Financial Supermarkets Incorporated, a painting that would be generic from coast to coast, one that would be interesting to all kinds of people. My first thought was how in the world could I do that in a painting?

I thought of what the bank stood for, and I thought of bartering in the old general stores. I thought that banks probably started in the old general stores. I knew that they had everything in there from the post office to the bank to the hardware store, from dry goods to produce and a meat market. That was what I started working on.

Then I put Mr. Wingate as the proprietor standing in the front with an apron on, handing out crackers and standing by the cracker barrel and the pickle barrel and just being friendly like he is. I wanted his total personality to show forth. I told him about my idea, and he said, "Go ahead and start."

I worked over it, drawing and redrawing until I was pleased and he was pleased. Every step of the way, he was never too busy to participate and enjoy every step, right through the printing. He wanted to know everything about it. He bought the copyright. He was a perfectionist about the details. He didn't let things slip, and that's the way it ought to be.

One thing that was important to him was having his little boys in the painting. I think the painting succeeds in that you can see what kind of man he is with his family and his children and the community, all in that painting right there. He wanted to serve and there he is serving, passing out crackers and being friendly. That's it in a nutshell for me. I could depend on him, and he could depend on me to do my best after that job.

Another painting he commissioned was a painting of where he was born.

I took photographs and did a little sketching and came home and got that painting finished, and he ended up with a painting of his home place.

He was my best customer. One time he said to me, "I'm just trying to help you." I knew that was true without him saying it. I could see that that's what he was about. That was it in a nutshell. He deserves our praise.

SEPTEMBER 2005

Attracting dollars and customers

THE COINSTAR PROJECT: AN EXAMPLE

RECENTLY WE SIGNED AN AGREEMENT WITH COINSTAR. The way it came about can serve as another example of how ideas become reality. When I started seeing Coinstar putting these machines in supermarkets five years ago, I said to myself, "You know, that's something banks should be doing because we're in the money business." As it turned out, there was an individual, two or three individuals, that did the research and found that there is ten billion dollars in loose coins out there, and they thought that what we need to do is bring those coins back into circulation. And when they did the studies of where do the customers go, they found out that the number one place was the supermarket. So I approached them and told them I'd like to talk to them about putting one of the machines in my bank.

I just picked up the phone and called them, told them who I was. I could tell that their main focus was retailers, so we never could get any place with them at that time. So I went out and bought a machine, not from Coinstar, but a regular machine and we offered it free to roll the customers' coins. I was reading about Coinstar and learned that they have 11,000 machines out there. So we put ours in. In Cornelia, Georgia, with that one machine we were attracting 70,000 dollars a month, 70,000 dollars a month coming in through that machine.

People would bring the coins in, and they were depositing sixty percent of the money and taking the other forty percent in cash. It was just mind-boggling. It took 750 customers to generate that kind of volume. That's 750 potential customers. And they were coming inside the bank as well.

When Coinstar had a change in management about three years ago, I went back to them. I'd been keeping track of them. And by this time I had proof as to what the machines would do in the bank.

It turns out they had tried to get something going in the banks, but they hadn't been able to. I told them about FSI and what our job is, that we call on banks to talk about in-store banking and we could just add that to our saddle bag and talk to the banks about Coinstar. They saw the value of FSI. That's when we signed the agreement.

So a year later, we should have, by the end of this year, over a hundred Coinstar installations in financial institutions. ■

Howard Hess (background), one of Alton's closest friends,
and another good friend, J. J. McKellar

CHAPTER FOURTEEN

New Frontiers: Horses, Hunting, Fishing, and Waffle House

WHEN I WAS A CHILD, WE HAD MULES; WE DIDN'T HAVE HORSES. And I loved riding horses, but Daddy never did have any horses on the farm, so I rode a mule. His name was Peanut. I made a comment to a friend here one day that I'd like to have 50 acres, and he said, "What do you want 50 acres for?"

I said, "I want to put some horses on it. But before I find the horses, I need to find me a cowboy to take care of them." He said, "Well, my wife and I will be the cowboy, and we've got the land, so all you need to do is buy the horses." So I'm in partnership with a couple in Banks County where I own the horses and they keep them up. There was a story in *Southern Living* about them recently. Their names are Doc and Nanette Sisk, and they're both SEC officials in basketball.

Those horses were the first that I bought. I go up there and ride.

* * * * *

In our home and in my office, I've gathered quite a few trophies, guns, and other mementos of a special aspect of my life that came to me, now that I look back, almost like a surprise, something that was not really

A boyhood dream comes true

part of my childhood or early adulthood – something, in a way, that my banking life brought me, well, that some of the friends I made through professional activities brought me to – and that is outdoor adventures.

Until I was 45 years old, I had only one gun, Dad's shotgun. Until then, Linda says all I did was work, and that's true. I didn't play golf or hunt or fish or any of those things. And I probably wouldn't have gotten going with the hunting and fishing if it hadn't come to me as part of work, as part of business development. I wouldn't have done it if I hadn't been able to do it with customers as a part of developing and continuing business relationships. But work and life have never been separate to me, so it seems like all of a piece. The men I went with on these trips –which I call stress-management meetings – are the men I consider my closest friends. I never could have justified the trips if it weren't for the business aspects.

Howard Hess, one of my closest friends, I met through a supermarket deal.

This all started in the late eighties. One place where we hunted was in Kingsville, Texas, at the King Ranch. It's 825,000 acres. It's the place that

Edna Ferber's book *Giant* is based on – and the movie and a TV series, too.

Every time I went to King Ranch, I was a guest of somebody else. We'd go out there for three or four days. You bring your own guns.

I've got pictures of the first deer I shot and pictures of my first turkey. And I have a picture of the first time Linda and I went fly fishing. (She'd say, "The first time I went, first and only.")

A guy named Andy Shepard is the one that exposed me to fly fishing. This was in Kremmling, Colorado, at Elktrout Lodge. Andy's a banker, and he'd invited a bunch of bankers out there. He lives in California, but he loves fly fishing; he and a couple of his directors built this lodge out there. And we'd go out there and play golf in the morning, fish in the afternoon. It's a wonderful place.

They had people there to help you if you didn't know how to do things. All you had to do was come with equipment. They had guides for

Linda and Alton at Elktrout Lodge in Kremmling, Colorado, 1998

Outdoor fun at Elktrout Lodge in Kremmling, Colorado. From left: Dave & Sandy Borrow, Dean & Kay Swanson, Jackie & Charles Sherwood, Linda & Alton Wingate

everybody. One guide for each person. So, I had my own guide.

I've gotten to go deep-sea fishing in Alaska and Louisiana. I'd never been to Alaska before I carried the three boys – Frank, Edward, and Beau – out there in 1998. It was a treat, having the boys out there for a week.

* * * * *

But as for hunting trips, when I was first invited to go on them, I'd never been on one before, and I had just regular shoes, a pair of blue jeans, and a shotgun Linda gave me, and that was it. Then Charles H. McKellar, executive vice president with Winn-Dixie stores, gave me a Remington 20 gauge automatic designed for upland bird hunting, and that was the beginning of it. I just kept going from there, until we had to build a room for them. Linda will tell you some of them are still stacked up around her on the floor and behind the door, under a bed.

What I got out of it personally was a lot more than I can really put into words. It was a pleasure getting up early in the morning – for instance, when we were hunting turkey – going out and sitting under a tree and hearing the birds start chirping. It's really hard to describe. It was peaceful, but so much more than that.

One of my favorite pictures from hunting trips is one Howard Hess took of me and the guide. It was pitch black dark, but it was so wonderful just sitting under that tree, hearing the birds chirp, hearing the world wake up.

Some people say, as to close friends, you can count them on one hand. I mean close friends. But what do you call a close friend? Well, a close friend, if your breath smells, he'll tell you. But there are probably

New frontiers bring new prizes

about five people, if you stop and think about it. That's about it. You might know a lot of people, but your closest friends will only be a few of those.

If I'd never met up with these guys, I never would want to shoot. I mean I had no desire to shoot. But that's all these guys did; they loved to hunt. I never would have gone out by myself and shot a deer.

* * * * *

I got into the Waffle House business just because the banking commissioner for the state of Georgia got into the Waffle House business. He helped them get started back in 1955. So they are fifty years old. Well, he loaned them the money when he was a banker. He wound up owning all of the Waffle Houses in North Carolina, and he got me into the Waffle House business about five years ago.

So, a long time ago, I got out of the tire business. I got out of the chicken business and got out of everything. The only thing I'm involved in now is Waffle House. But I have someone who takes care of them for me. ■

From left: Marvin, Stokley, and Alton Wingate, with sisters, from left, Veda Wingate Tison and Sarah Wingate Johnson

J. Alton Wingate, President & CEO

CHAPTER FIFTEEN

CAPITAL IS A VERY PRECIOUS WORD & OTHER THOUGHTS

I'VE ALWAYS BELIEVED IN TEAMWORK. You know, I've been able to build this company: that's my first team; those are the people I work for. I've tried to surround myself with quality people, and I kind of act as a coach, you might say. And it's a team effort. We've got a big family here; we had 18 employees when I came here, and I think now we've got over 450 employees company-wide.

What I've been able to do here has been because of the people who have worked with me. It has been a case of just take a dream and build on it. I enjoy giving more than receiving, and I've been very blessed, very blessed. My board has supported me on everything that I have presented to them, and I know from other banker friends that that is not always the case. I promised my board that I'd never surprise them, that I'd always try to keep them informed, and, likewise, I expected the same thing from them. And we've just had a wonderful relationship.

People have been so kind to me, telling me I've touched a lot of lives, but I consider us a team and a family here. I'm just trying to think about the community. I have always felt like I've been very lucky, and I want to give back to the community because of what it has given to me as an individual.

I believe in education and health care, that it just makes sense that those are the ingredients that help make a community a good place to live and work and raise a family. We started off as a bank, and we've added a lot of things, ways of helping people, of building the community.

* * * * *

The key before any small business gets started is capital; it takes capital, no matter what the business. Any business starts off as a community business. A large metropolitan company starts off as a small community business, and then it grows. Some companies remain private all the way through, and normally some go public. The prime reason for a company to go public is to raise capital. Capital is a very precious word, a precious word.

Also, of course, you've got to make money; if you don't make money, you're not going to be around. For each business that you have, once you write your business plan, you can be sure that more than likely all of your business plan that you have so carefully outlined will change within two or three years. That's because once you start out, you'll find out that it's a little bit different than what you thought it was going to be, and you have to be flexible and be willing to change. If I had to say what's the most important ingredient in starting a business, it would be being able to raise capital and having enough capital to fulfill your business plan. That would be my recommendation to any business.

* * * * *

Personal finance is very important, and today personal finance is probably more important than ever before because of technology. So many products and services are being offered based on an individual's credit rating. You know if you've got a credit rating here, normally the lower your rating is, the more you're going to have to pay for money because the risk is greater. And when the risk is greater, that's when you have to pay more for money.

I was in the credit card business in the early '60's – I was with C & S then – when it became apparent that that was a way the consumers would like to charge. The biggest problem that we had then was getting people to understand how the credit card worked, that you have to make a payment every single month, that if your payment's twenty dollars and you pay forty, you can't skip the next month.

It seems like our world is in disarray in terms of how people's minds work regarding credit. A lot of our customers then thought (and people today think) that they could skip the next month if they had paid more than required the month before. It doesn't work that way. It was an education for me to see how many people thought that it did.

Credit today is easier to get than ever before. America has been hit by so many bankruptcies, and that's why we've been hearing about bankruptcy reform. And it needs to be reformed because it was too easy for people to file for bankruptcy. When a person files for bankruptcy, we can't help them for at least seven years. I think the reason so many people have filed for bankruptcy is lack of education on how you use credit, and

Treating people like you like to be treated is very important. And so is recognizing the importance of education.

they've just got debts running out their ears, and they are unable to service the debt.

But America is built on credit. Sixty percent of automobiles are financed. Ninety percent of houses are financed. And look how many credit cards people have access to today, where it used to be maybe one or none. Now there's one, there's two, there's three, there's four. They just keep piling up. People need to recognize that credit is a privilege. It's nothing that you're entitled to; it's a privilege. And if you abuse that privilege, you the individual have to pay the consequences. That's basically the way it works.

* * * * *

I think that the advantages of growing up in a Christian home can make all the difference in a person's life. My philosophy has always been to do your best at what you do, no matter what you do. Set your goals and set those goals so that they can be achieved. But whatever goals you may be setting, do your best.

Treating people like you like to be treated is very important. And so is recognizing the importance of education. Education is so important today, and it is a different level than what it was when I came along. I mean, of course, especially computer science: the computers we have today are just the tip of the iceberg as to what you're going to be seeing down the road. Communication has changed so much. Just think about telephones. I can remember when you just picked up the phone and gave the operator a number, and you only had five minutes to talk. And there were other people on the line, the party line. Now I use a cell phone. Who would have ever thought ten years ago that cell phones would be like they are today. Just ten years ago. Just ten years.

Of course, technological advances affect banking, too. I think banking ten or twenty years from now is going to be more electronically driven, but I don't think that we're going to get to the point where we do away with the human touch. I just do not feel that banking will get that technology driven.

* * * * *

To sum it up, I had to be born with this in me, it was in my DNA. But I enjoyed helping people, making people feel good, making a sale of something that somebody really wanted, convincing them how it could help them. It's just like I've been in the business of helping people all my life, doing the paper route, selling stuff to them.

Thinking over the past in order to work on this book, going back and looking at the laundry list of things that I have done, it has kind of amazed me, how many things I've been involved in. I never had thought of it.

You know what prepared me for the bank? The paper route, with my little-over-600 customers. It taught me the value of a dollar and how to meet people. That's what it took. The banking business is a relationship business. Banks today are different than they were ten years ago. They're almost like daylight and dark different, from the sixties to the year 2005. It's because of so many changes. Technology has driven a lot of changes, as did deregulation, but our bank has managed to thrive.

A lot of banks have not. We've come from fifteen thousand banks to ten thousand. And the reason for that is all the mergers and acquisitions that have gone on. A lot of community banks have given up, have said we can't compete. But that's what's so unique about our bank. From our shareholders to our board of directors to our management team, we all have been committed to our goals.

My board said that we'd like to remain a community bank, and that's all I've tried to do: build a stronger community bank. We've never had to go out and raise capital because we always made enough money to maintain our capital growth. I give all the credit to my people that I've been fortunate to have been able to hire over the years.

I think there's always going to be a place for a community bank. Always. ■

ALTON WINGATE:
ENTHUSIASM AND SINCERITY

BY DENNIS CATHEY

Founding Partner: Cathey & Strain, Attorneys

Do you remember when you first met Alton and what you thought of him?

Well, when I first met Alton, he was a young banker who had come in to town. And interestingly, I didn't bank with him then. I banked with another bank; he never solicited me directly to be a customer of the bank. He was just friendly, outgoing, and enthusiastic. We met each other socially a few times.

When I moved into my new office, he greatly encouraged me to do that and was really touting helping downtown Cornelia. He was instrumental in people being aware of the new downtown development authority we had going. So he encouraged me to improve an old building in the downtown area, and my banking relationship with him started. We'd already been socially good friends; the friendship would have grown more then had I not had a business relationship with him. I think it's more coincidental because we just shared a lot of the same thoughts, a lot of the same ideals. And so I remember him as being a very, very strong advocate of our town.

Of course, I went to church with him. Back when I met him I didn't have any children, so like a lot of young marrieds, I wasn't going to church very much. But when I started having kids, I started going to church more. He was already a member of my church, the church my wife grew up in. So the big three-legged stool – social interaction here in town, the banking world, and our church and the community – we just were thrown together in all three of those things. The more I got to know him, the better I liked him. I guess that's what happens with your friends.

Would you agree that he seems to have the entrepreneurial gene?

I've thought about that and thought about him when he was a young paper-boy throwing the paper and running his paper route for money in Albany, Georgia, riding his bicycle. That paperboy ended up being an international entrepreneur. But that little boy riding the bicycle part never changed. He still was the little boy riding the bicycle. So there were two components of Alton; they started there when he was young and always stayed the same.

Oh, that's a great way to put it.

His bicycle later became his Harley-Davidson and his paper route became Financial Supermarkets Incorporated. So it was, he never changed; he still had that. He was an entrepreneur, but he always had a lot of playful, good-natured joy to him.

And now he's riding horses.

He's always liked the outdoors and horses and cowboys and things of that nature. That's part of that little boy; when you're a little boy, you always want to ride the horse.

That's a great detail; that does help capture the charm of him.

And he loves the West. He loves going out to fish for trout in Colorado, and it's a little bit more upscale fishing out there at the resort. They loved him out there, and he likes going. He obviously enjoys travel, seeing different parts of the world, but it's meeting people too.

And from what he said about when he started into the hunting and fishing, that's been an added grace note to his life. He really wouldn't have started into it the way that he did without feeling that it was good for the business, too, but he talks quite eloquently at times and always excitedly about some of those things. He said, "In my Argentina trip that was taken with Dennis Cathey, I've never seen so many doves in my life; four of us shot seven thousand."

We shot until we couldn't shoot anymore. And let me tell you a little more about that trip.

Okay, good.

Me, my partner, Ed Strain, Howard Hess, and Alton. You've heard Howard's name; he's told you all about that. We planned the trip to Argentina. Now Ed and I had been going – it was not our first trip to that lodge, but it was the first trip there for Alton and Howard. So we set it all up through our outfitter, and as Alton is wont to do, when the time came to go – the day before – he has a conflict, so he's not going to be able to travel with us; he's going to come down a day later.

Of course, he's hurry-scurry getting all his ducks in a row for his obligation, whatever it was that meant he couldn't come with us. So I, having been on this international hunting trip all the way to Argentina before, said, "Now, Alton, this is the deal," and I explained the arrangements. Well, I didn't know how much of that sunk in. All he wanted to know, he said, "Now, somebody's going to meet me at the airport, right?"

"Yes," I said, "somebody's going to meet you at the airport with a car." I

also told him other details, but that's all the part that really sunk in. So when he gets to the airport, sure enough our outfitter on the ground meets him.

"Where's my rental car?" Alton says.

"No, Mr. Wingate, we're going to have somebody drive you to the lodge." Although I had told him, he's forgotten how far it is. So he thinks he's going to jump in and that it's one of these high-falutin' lodges that he goes to, that you drive 15 minutes and there's the lodge.

Actually, it's five hours from Buenos Aires to the lodge. After about 30 minutes, he starts talking to the driver. "How much farther to the lodge?" he asks. About that time, he figures out that it might be difficult to communicate in that he can't speak a word of Spanish, and the driver doesn't speak a word of English. The driver doesn't know what the heck Alton's saying to him. Alton continues trying to talk to him, and all he can get out of the driver is a nod and a smile. That's the response, time and again. After three or four hours, Alton assumes he's been kidnapped.

Sure.

So, when Alton finally arrives and I rendezvous with him, I get the biggest bear hug of my life, and he says he's never been so glad to see anybody in his life. Well, I hadn't heard his story yet, but I said, "Alton, I love seeing you, too."

But we had a delightful weekend – well, a few days in the lodge – and I really got to know Howard a lot better on that trip; it was just a real bonding experience for all of us, and it was a fun, fun trip. Of course, though, this is Alton Wingate, and he doesn't stop being Alton Wingate just because we're out in the middle of nowhere. He's so interested in financial supermarkets, he asks about grocery stores. "Alton," I said, "you've got more in your suitcase than any grocery store within a hundred miles of here."

And, of course, he's always seeing stuff in these other locales that interests him. And so, the gauchos down there had this, over their saddle they throw this fleece, you know just a raw piece of sheep fleece, that they put on the saddle as their cushion. Well, nothing would deter Alton, he had to buy one of those down there and bring it back. I think it's hanging around the bank or somewhere; he had to have a fleece like the gauchos had. So, once again, he found a cowboy accouterment that he had to buy when he saw one. It was like an old dog bed. Anyway, if it's good enough for gauchos, it's good enough for Alton.

I can just see him telling the grocers how they could have a bank in their store.

Right. And on our trips to South Dakota, the first time we went to South Dakota hunting pheasants together, well, they'd opened one of the gigantic Cabela's stores there at Mitchell, South Dakota, where we go. I don't know if you're familiar with Cabela's, but it's L.L Bean and Bass Pro Shop squared, just the biggest mail order thing. Well, you talk about somebody in Toys "R" Us, he goes into Cabela's, and he buys a cap for everybody. It's not good enough for him to buy just his own cap; he buys all four of us a cap. And when he comes out of there, it's like a clown act: he's got beef jerky, he's got peanuts, he's got gloves, he's got head scarves, he's got headbands, he's got all these orange khaki things he buys and a big orange cowboy hat.

So he really had fun with those things.

Oh, yeah. And when you travel with him, it's like the Czar going to the summer palace or Teddy Roosevelt on his post-presidential safari to Africa. We went hunting one time for I think three days, and I think I counted seven pairs of boots that he packed. He is just bigger than life; everything he does is just full of vigor and full of exuberance and full of enthusiasm, punctuated by laughing and that big old garrulous laugh of his and the way he just bends over and squints those eyes and laughs. He's just the greatest.

And so generous.

He's the softest touch in the world. He is totally selfless. He is one of the most unselfish people, if not the most unselfish and kindest and considerate people you will ever see. And some people misconstrue that. Some people see just the business side of him, which is very protective of his stockholders and his employees. He takes very, very seriously his fiduciary obligation to the stockholders in his bank. And on the other side, it almost looks like he would be a skinflint because he's so protective of his bank, but that's because he honors his responsibilities. He considers himself a steward of people's money and their stock in the bank. But in his own personal world, he'll give you the shirt off his back. Literally.

He talked a lot about his father and how his father took care of people in their community.

He inherited that from his father. He has the ability to judge who needs help, and he is kind enough to do what he can. He's just an unbelievable person.

He will not talk about the generosity and kindness that other people always mention about him.

That's a part of him, that's exactly what I would anticipate. But Howard Hess probably told you – I've heard him say this about Alton – he said, "You don't know how many hundred-dollar handshakes I've seen him give people."

And Howard's right. I don't know how many hundred-dollar handshakes I've seen him give people. And good to children. I think he's just a big old child himself. He's just a big old boy, and it was real funny when he used to call my office and sternly ask, "Dennis there?" It would just intimidate the heck out of the receptionist: "Dennis there?" And then he'd come in here, and it was easy to see just what a big old teddy bear he is. Funny as the dickens. His bark is a lot worse than his bite. He wasn't being rude; he just was to the point.

And this is the man who provides the town with popcorn and shoe-shines.

Popcorn and shoe shines, what else can I say?

From your vantage point as a person in Cornelia, what's your sense of what Financial Supermarkets, Incorporated (FSI) is all about and what it has done for the bank and the shareholders?

Well, first of all, it is such a visionary thing he did. And, you know, it's tough to be a prophet in your own land. And I don't know if everybody fully grasped the significance of what his bank and FSI have meant to the community, but they have provided jobs and put us on the map. You don't go anywhere and mention Cornelia, Georgia, that somebody doesn't say, "Do you know Mr. Wingate?" I think he considers FSI his legacy in the business world.

Yes, yes.

And it's just a product of a couple of things. One, his novel visionary concept of what he wanted. And the other is his ability; you can lay every bit of success at the feet of his personal relationships with people. He went out and sold this on the strength of himself and the force of his personality. I believe that. He created this thing, but had somebody else come up with the idea without the eclectic mix of special characteristics he had, I don't think it could've been done. Where does somebody get off hiring a company from a town of five thousand to do a project like this?

Right.

And once he got established here, he never wanted to be anywhere but right here in Cornelia, Georgia, doing this. It was seductive to have an Atlanta address, I'm sure, when he started this. It would have been easy to say we've got to get credibility by going somewhere else; it never entered his mind to do it anywhere but right here in this town.

And he believed in it so strongly as he built it. Failure didn't have a chance.

His enthusiasm is infectious, it really is. His enthusiasm, you can tell it. There are two things that you can tell about Alton Wingate immediately, and they are qualities you look for when you're in litigation. They are what juries look for. One is enthusiasm. The other is sincerity.

Definitely.

And a third one that, of course, anybody can have is the expertise. But those other two, enthusiasm and sincerity, are more important than expertise. And an important part of what he did required those qualities because he had to make people believe in this thing.

Right.

And as far as his character in a small town, I've told him before that if Cornelia hadn't had him, we would have had to invent him. He was an absolute necessity for the growth and the viability of this little town. Of course, you can't even talk about his being just a Cornelia enterprise; he's all over.

Right. FSI is literally all over the map. And he puts the depiction of the old-fashioned grocery store – the one that shows the market and post office and bank all in one place – in every new unit FSI opens.

Yes, they have got them everywhere. But let me tell you, my oldest child is 24. When Alton was first starting his venture he took a picture of my wife and my son, who was then three, and that became the cover of his brochure. And I still have it. And years later when they opened, I don't know, store number so-and-so, he had a little ceremony, and he gave my son like ten bucks for every one of those stores that had opened. Alton thanked him, saying, "You were our cover boy when this started." It was several thousand dollars.

Oh, wasn't that nice.

Several thousand bucks. And it's still in a CD in Community Bank and Trust. So that's the kind of thing Alton does – totally unexpected. Totally unexpected and it meant so much to Matt. Honest to Pete, it was unex-

pected; I think he was ready to go off to college at that time.

Those are the kind of things he does, but his enthusiasm sometimes doesn't work out that well. For instance, we went on a trip to New York City, two or three couples. On all of these trips Alton either meets somebody that tells him something or he's got a business card from somebody at some restaurant or some limo driver; it doesn't have to be a person of prestige. It can be "Get your shoes shined by this guy," or "Look, this is the cab driver you want." He just collects all this stuff from all these places he goes. So he said, "We've got to ride in one of those double-decker buses, take a tour of the city in one of those open-topped red buses." And it was just his enthusiasm that made us agree to go. Well, we got tired of the bus ride real quick – all of us did, even him – and we said, "Alton, we appreciate your enthusiasm; this is a great trip, but we've about had it."

His enthusiasm is powerful. You've got to be careful or you'll sign on to everything he wants to do.

It sounds like he was hands-on with everything as he built FSI.

Total immersion into the project, hands on in every aspect. By the same token, very quick to listen to other people's ideas. Very quick to speak to people with expertise. But that's what makes a great leader. He did those things, but was very engaged himself.

He did manage to figure out how to do it, judging by the results.

He was the strategist. He left the tactics sometimes to other people, but the great strategical design was his.

And then, of course, you know all of that opened up other channels

that he figured out how to leverage, Coinstar, for instance.

Coinstar, those things open up, contacts with ability to purchase other banks. Ability to come in with something national like Coinstar. That was out there for anybody that wanted to do that. Why didn't anybody do that? There's a stream of people using those Coinstars everywhere.

Yes.

He had that ability to see, recognize the potential, and do that project.

And there was a lot of strategy there because first they weren't interested and he waited and he watched and then when he saw his opportunity – that kind of thing might make him a good hunter.

There are certain elements in his life he has patience in and certain other elements that he doesn't have patience in. When we first got on the dove field – and maybe if you don't hunt, you can't appreciate it – here's a story from when we first got in the dove field in Argentina, In Georgia, in the states, you have a shotgun; it's not permitted to shoot more than three times. You can make an adjustment in South America and can shoot five times. So he sits down and the first bird he sees, it sounds like Baghdad: dah-dah-dah-dah-dah. He empties his gun and here flies the bird on down and away. If he could have been a little patient and got a little closer, he would have gotten it. But you know what, this was the first time he'd ever used that shotgun. But what told me something about him was the fact that, by the time that trip ended, he was a crack shot.

Really.

Crack shot. Yes. No patience at the beginning. When he emptied that shotgun, it really sounded like it was a sub-machine gun. But by the time the trip was over, dead eye.

Wow. Well, just another thing on that trip, a person who's used to the pace of business that he is, for him to be in that five-hour ride, especially with the uncertainty. It's just so hard to imagine him sitting still for that long.

And then we get in a lodge where there's no telephone; there's no e-mail. He had no choice but to relax for a few days.

Right.

And we just had an excellent time, a real ball. I look back at it and chuckle about it every day of my life.

Let's see. Any other of your trips that you would like to mention or special.

Well, that's about it, that's the highlights, New York, South America. We'd been pheasant hunting, but that's in the states so we've done that often. And one year we had to wait to go on our hunt while he talked to the Governor on a conference call. We got used to those kind of things. He said he had an important conference call. We're all going to breakfast, and I start ribbing him about his conference call: "What's more important than hunting with me and the guys?"

"Well," he began, and I said, "Come on, what is it? You got somebody that's opening a bank in Hoboken or what's going on?"

"Well, actually," he said, "I am on some board, and I've got to talk with the Governor."

"I'll let you off the hook this time," I said.

So we had those kind of things going on all the time. He has met a lot of interesting and important people. But I've observed him with that cab driver, and I've observed him with elected officials, and there's one Alton Wingate.

That echoes something he said about his father and how his father treated people.

And he's the same fellow that rolled into this town as a young banker and worked hard trying to find a way to make money in the tire business and whatever else he had going, and he's the very same guy who's now fabulously successful. And he's the same Alton, sticking out that hand and saying, "Hey, partner." Same guy.

Would you like to say anything about your Saturday mornings that you have with him sometimes?

Well, I always know he's in the bank working Saturday mornings, most mornings, and it's a time I can go in to see him and we can talk about some things. It's never planned; it's just a time to go by. I always feel welcome, and we can always talk. I never know what we are going to talk about when I get there, and that's what friends do. It's just our time to talk and, you know, you kind of have a meter that you know when somebody's too busy to see you, a good time or not a good time. But I enjoy stopping by to see him, and it is just usually a lot of laughs, and we catch up on what we call the gossip. Mostly state politics or local happenings. It's just fun. And we talk about our children and what is going on in our lives and often plan to go to dinner that night or something.

The true community bank.

The true community bank. He always gives me a cup of coffee; they are just fine times. He is such a good person to bounce things off of. He is just a good person to talk with about anything in your life, anything that is going on. He is always interested. You always know he is interested. He isn't just going through the motions of listening to you.

Alton's life transcends the business world. Now you know in Norman McClain's book A River Runs Through It, *he said, "In our family there was never a clear-cut division between religion and fly fishing." There has never been a clear-cut division in Alton's life between his business and his community and having fun. So it kind of runs together for him. He's just unusual in his ability to make all that work together so well. As great a business man as he is, I think a lot more about him as a person than about him in his business world. And I think that's a great compliment.*

It is a great compliment.

His business world was just a given. I know that's going to be successful, and, of course, I'm a shareholder in Community Bank and Trust, so I get all the mail outs and I know what's going on, but I didn't have to pay much attention because I know he has it all together. The business success is a given.

I think it goes, once again, back to that young paperboy throwing the paper and running his paper route for money in Albany, Georgia, riding his bicycle. That paperboy ended up being an international entrepreneur. The generous, enthusiastic and sincere man he became, the one who has brought so much to our community, still has all the heart of that little boy riding the bicycle. I am proud to call him my friend.

JULY 28, 2005

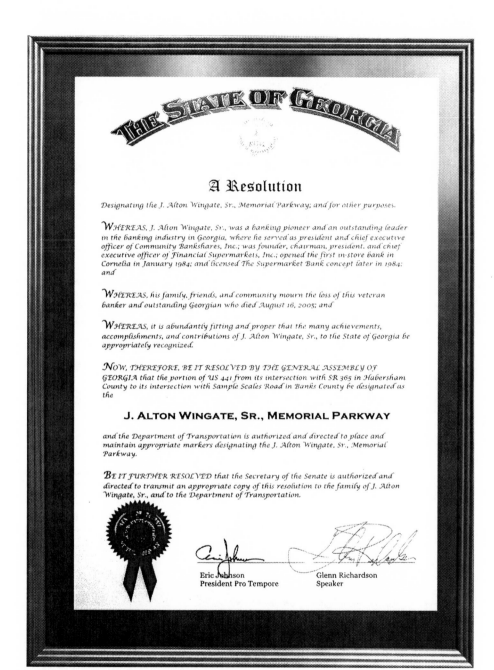

THE STATE OF GEORGIA

A Resolution

Designating the J. Alton Wingate, Sr., Memorial Parkway; and for other purposes.

WHEREAS, J. Alton Wingate, Sr., was a banking pioneer and an outstanding leader in the banking industry in Georgia, where he served as president and chief executive officer of Community Bankshares, Inc.; was founder, chairman, president, and chief executive officer of Financial Supermarkets, Inc.; opened the first in-store bank in Cornelia in January 1984; and licensed The Supermarket Bank concept later in 1984; and

WHEREAS, his family, friends, and community mourn the loss of this veteran banker and outstanding Georgian who died August 16, 2005; and

WHEREAS, it is abundantly fitting and proper that the many achievements, accomplishments, and contributions of J. Alton Wingate, Sr., to the State of Georgia be appropriately recognized.

NOW, THEREFORE, BE IT RESOLVED BY THE GENERAL ASSEMBLY OF GEORGIA that the portion of US 441 from its intersection with SR 365 in Habersham County to its intersection with Sample Scales Road in Banks County be designated as the

J. ALTON WINGATE, SR., MEMORIAL PARKWAY

and the Department of Transportation is authorized and directed to place and maintain appropriate markers designating the J. Alton Wingate, Sr., Memorial Parkway.

BE IT FURTHER RESOLVED that the Secretary of the Senate is authorized and directed to transmit an appropriate copy of this resolution to the family of J. Alton Wingate, Sr., and to the Department of Transportation.

Eric Johnson
President Pro Tempore

Glenn Richardson
Speaker

Georgia honors Alton

ROY E. BARNES
P O BOX 161
MABLETON, GEORGIA 30126

July 29, 2005

Alton

As I reminisce over the many years of our friendship, I smile.
I smile because everytime I see you a funny thing happened.
Like the time we were at the Community Bankers meeting and you rode that little moped everywhere. A big man on a small moped, especially with it being Alton Wingate, still brings a smile to my face.

But the biggest smile is what you have given back to your community. You always gave back. I only wish we had more Alton Wingates everywhere. This would be such a better place.

A letter from a favorite friend, former Governor Roy Barnes

ROY E. BARNES
P O BOX 161
MABLETON, GEORGIA 30126

– 2 –

But the greatest smile
would be in remembering
your friendship. I will
never forget you old
friend, across all time
and space; under all
conditions. Your friendship
is something I shall
always treasure.

Roy

ACKNOWLEDGEMENTS

From the very beginning and throughout my life, I have been so blessed. I was born into a loving and supportive family: My parents, James Leonard and Ida Lois Hatcher Wingate; and my brothers and sisters, Marvin (Jack) and James Stokley Wingate and Veda W. Tison and Sarah W. Johnson.

My beloved wife, Linda Hodgkinson Wingate; our sons Frank, Edward, and Joseph Alton Wingate, Jr. (Beau); and our grandchildren, Caroline, Anna Lea, Meredith, Carlin, Elizabeth, and Joseph Alton Wingate, III continued that love and support and not only completed my life, but made it worthwhile.

Throughout my career at Community Bank and Trust in Cornelia, Annette Fricks, who began as a valued assistant and is now a member of the holding company board, has been very important to any success I have achieved. In addition, the many employees of Community Bank and Trust and Financial Supermarkets, Inc. have meant more to me than I could ever express. I thank each and every one of them.

The boards of directors I have served have given me guidance, support, and the gift of their experience and wisdom. While I can't name them all here, I would like to name, in honor of all of my board members, the members of the one I currently report to, in 2005: H. Calvin Stovall, Chairman of the Board; Steven C. Adams, Edwin B. Burr, Annette R. Fricks, Dean C. Swanson, George D. Telford, A. Dan Windham, M.D., and Lois Wood-Schroyer. In the same spirit, I would like to name the 2005 officers, in honor of all those who served as officers during my tenure with

Community Bank and Trust: Edwin B. Burr, Annette R. Fricks, Harry L. Stephens, Wesley A. Dodd, Jr., William M. Galardi, William S. Loyd, Marlon R. Mayfield, James G. W. Mullis, Michael Dunagan, Wendell L. Fincannon, Linda T. Smart, Michael J. Barden, Jan C. Garrison, Jeffrey J. Webb, Deanna Mote, Mary P. Wilkinson, Denver Gunn, and Deborah Hudson.

Indeed, I have been blessed with family, colleagues, employees, and board members. In addition, throughout my life, mentors and friends have appeared as well to share the journey, the work, and the fun. Some of your names are mentioned in this book; so many are not. Because it would not be possible to name each one of you, I will here thank every one of you and say, "Bless you, partner. Your guidance and friendship have meant the world to me. You have helped to make my world and my life truly wonderful."

J. Alton Wingate

PROFESSIONAL

Chairman, President and CEO of Community Bankshares, Inc. an interstate, multi-bank holding company with corporate headquarters in Cornelia, Georgia. Community Bankshares, Inc. is a three-bank financial holding company whose consolidated assets are close to one billion dollars. The consolidated assets of Community Bankshares, and its non-bank subsidiaries now include (in addition to Financial Supermarkets, Inc.): Financial Solutions, a financial consulting firm; Financial Properties (Century 21 Community Realty); Community Travel Services; and Community Insurance Services, Inc.

Banking career spanned 45 years.

Founder and president of Financial Supermarkets, Inc., parent company of The Supermarket Bank. Pioneer of in-store banking in both the United States and Europe. He was referred to by many in banking circles as the Father of Supermarket Banking.

SELECTED MEMBERSHIPS AND HONORS

Named one of the nation's outstanding bank CEOs by Banker's Monthly Magazine.

Served as president of the Georgia Bankers Association and was chairman emeritus of the Bankers Board of the Conference of State Bank Supervisors (CSBS).

A past member of the Bank Administration Institute (BAI) Board of Directors, most recently he served on the President's Council of the BAI in 1999.

First recipient of the Georgia Bankers Association's Chairman's Leadership Award for his outstanding service to the financial services industry in the State of Georgia.

In 2004, the Northeast Georgia Council of the Boy Scouts of America honored Mr. Wingate at an American Values Dinner with its Distinguished Citizenship Award.

Also in 2004, Appalachian Community Enterprises, Inc., an organization which promotes entrepreneurship and provides loans, training and technical support for expanding micro enterprise named its annual Workhorse Award in Mr. Wingate's honor.

A native of Albany, Georgia, Wingate attended Georgia Southwestern College and the University of Georgia.

He served on the Georgia Bar Association's Fee Arbitration Committee, was named to Georgia's Cities Foundation, the Georgia Rural Development Council, the State Road and Toll Authority, and the Board of Directors of the Georgia Chamber of Commerce.

Civic organizations included the Habersham County Rotary Club (past president and Paul Harris fellow, the Board of Habersham County Medical Center, and the Board of Trustees of Piedmont College. Past chairman of the Habersham County Chamber of Commerce and co-founder of the Habersham County Fair Association.

Held virtually every lay leadership position in the Cornelia United Methodist Church. Chaired several financial campaigns, which retired debt on new construction, secured new facilities for an Hispanic ministry, and acquired property for future church expansion. Was the driving force behind the church's extremely successful endowment program.

PERSONAL

Born in Dougherty County, Georgia, on April 8, 1939.

Parents were James Leonard and Ida Lois Hatcher Wingate. Siblings included two brothers and two sisters: Marvin (Jack) Wingate (deceased), James Stokley Wingate, Veda W. Tison, and Sarah W. Johnson.

Wife, Linda Hodgkinson Wingate; three sons, Frank, Edward, and Joseph Alton Wingate, Jr. (Beau). Grandchildren, Caroline, Anna Lea, Meredith, Carlin, Elizabeth, and Joseph Alton Wingate, III.

Financial Supermarkets, Inc. (FSI) Fact Sheet

HISTORY

In January of 1984, FSI founder J. Alton Wingate opened the first Supermarket Bank® for Community Bank & Trust in Ingles Supermarket in Cornelia, Georgia.

In May 1984, FSI became the first company to license the in-store banking concept: The Supermarket Bank®.

In 2006, FSI has achieved 68% penetration in the continental United States, with institutions in 34 states partnering with FSI to provide in-store banking services.

PARTNERSHIPS

Strategic partnerships have been developed with Food Marketing Institute (FMI) and Coinstar. The Food Marketing Institute (FMI) chose Financial Supermarkets, Inc. as their preferred provider for customized private label in-store financial services. This endorsement of FSI offers FMI's members a complete package of design, fabrication, installation, marketing, training and operations for financial centers in supermarkets.

In 2004, FSI and Coinstar, Inc. formed a joint venture to provide self-service coin counting to financial institutions.

Retail partners include Albertson's, Bi-Lo, Bruno's, Food City, Fred Meyer, Harris Teeter, Hy-Vee, IGA, Ingles, Kroger, Safeway, Wal-Mart, and Winn-Dixie.

FEATURES

The Supermarket Bank® is custom-designed and built specifically for each retail environment. The full-service financial center averages approximately 400 to 700 square feet of space; however, designs have ranged from 100 to over 11,000 square feet. A 45,000 square-foot store need only dedicate 1/100th of its floor space for the financial center, which is often placed near the store entrance along with other new services such as video rentals or pharmacy.

The Supermarket Bank® has a cross-trained staff that delivers a variety of financial services and products. The financial center's staff then has the opportunity to interact with as many as 10,000 to 30,000 potential customers per week as they shop the financial center's 30-to-70,000 square foot "lobby."

The Supermarket Bank®, including equipment, furniture, and security systems, with staff can be installed for 1/5th the cost of a traditional brick and mortar branch. The new in-store financial center can usually be in operation within 75 days after an agreement is signed.

FSI's turnkey package is supported by ongoing consulting services.

STAFF

FSI staff includes bankers and retailers that provide advice and consultation, facility designers, project managers, marketing specialists, and sales trainers.

INDEX

A

B

C

Dunagan, Michael 135
Dunn, Jack 92

E

Elktrout Lodge 103, 104
Europe 71, 89, 136

F

father of supermarket banking xvi, 136
Financial Properties 136
Financial Solutions 136
Financial Supermarkets Incorporated (see also FSI) 71, 80, 84, 93, 117, 122, 134, 136, 140
Fincannon, Wendell I. 135
Food City 140
France 71, 86
Fred Meyer 140
Fricks, Annette R. 67, 134, 135
FSI (See also Financial Supermarkets, Incorporated) xi, 71, 80, 85, 86, 89, 90, 98, 122, 123, 124, 125, 140, 141

G

Galardi, William M. 135
Garrison, Jan C. 135
Georgia Bankers Association 45, 71, 136, 137
Georgia Banking Commission 92
Georgia Bar Association 137
Georgia Chamber of Commerce 137
Georgia's Cities Foundation 137
Georgia Rural Development Council 137
Georgia Southwestern College 42, 137
Gray, James (Jim) 13, 43
Grit 1, 2, 3
Gunn, Denver 135

H

I

J

K

outside adjuster 43, 49, 52, 55

P

Q

R

S

Workhorse Award 137

Worth County, Georgia 19

Wymer, Wymers' Lodge 36

Wingate, J. Alton xi, xv, xvi, xvii, xxii, 15, 30, 51, 56, 57, 62, 70, 71, 75, 82, 93, 94, 104, 107, 108, 116, 119, 120, 123, 128, 136, 140

Printed in the United States
84492LV00004BC/4-36/A

9 780977 336524